Kayak Isle Royale

A CALL TO YOUR WILD SOUL

Juniper Lauren Ross

ISBN: 979-8-9855774-0-2

This book is dedicated to Geneva White and Ava Kovach, women who live their Isle Royale dreams.

"What is it you plan to do with your one wild and precious life?"

Mary Oliver

TABLE OF CONTENTS

Disclaimer

Isle Royale has pulled me back for over thirty years to kayak her shores, sprawl on her beaches, and plunge into her frigid water. I hope to inspire you, dear reader, to build your own relationship with this place I love.

Along with the pleasures, however, there are dangers associated with kayaking Isle Royale. Lake Superior's cold water magnifies those risks. Her weather spins on a dime. Serious situations can occur anywhere: on the water, at the dock, on landing, on launching, or on a hiking trail. Isle Royale's remoteness amplifies potential consequences of injury or illness. Weather, lake conditions, the capacities of you and your party, and fate's dice will determine your exposure and the quality of your experience. Be careful. Pay attention. Know your limits and the limits of everyone in your group.

I am not medically or legally trained and nothing in this book is medical or legal advice. If you have questions in these areas, consult a professional. Schedule a checkup before any long trip.

The information in this book was accurate, to the best of my knowledge, at the time I wrote it. But trails, campgrounds, and conditions change. This guidebook cannot replace current charts and topographic maps, training, attention to your environment, planning, and good judgment. Almost anyone who wants to can plan and execute a safe and enjoyable Isle Royale kayaking experience. But the responsibility for your safety lies with you.

Introduction

Paddling is a practice not just for navigating lakes, oceans, shores, and landings, but for navigating life. Paddling is where I train for everything.

In each of us there is a desire to expand our world. To know ourselves and become more than who we are. Maybe you've read stories of Earnest Shackleton's incredible Antarctic adventures. Or of Kenton Grua, Rudy Petschek, and Steve Reynolds' epic race through the Grand Canyon in *The Emerald Mile.* Your high school copy of Walden, its underlined passages now half-forgotten, may still haunt you.

This book is based on the idea that paddling into a space between billion-year-old cliffs and the wave cresting right now can stretch our lives against a contracting girdle of safety. That we can move out of our comfort zone into our adventure zone. You may be busy from sunrise to sunset in cozy routines, ruts you've cut over decades. Student loans, children, jobs, or a mortgage might grind you down. And when you've outgrown those, you'll ask yourself if you're too old to go. But life wants to know from all of us what it is we dare to do.

In this book, I've proposed three Isle Royale paddling adventures. I've included tools to help you choose the one that is right for you. On any of these journeys, you'll meet sunlight's sparkle on Lake Superior's clear water. You'll ride a ferry across a distance that cannot be measured in miles. I've invited you to run your fingers over the weathered wood of a boat resting where it was hauled out a half century ago. To admire a wooden spool still draped with cotton threads of fishing nets. To experience an increasingly rare disconnection from all communication other than a human voice.

When you come, you'll meet those of us who cannot stay away. An ex-marine circumnavigated Isle Royale many summers in his twelve-foot recreational boat. Jerry, from Chelmsford, Massachusetts, has hiked every trail, dropped his canoe in most of Isle Royale's lakes, and kayaked her shores over twenty-seven years. Names inscribe shelter walls above a list of years. Stories scrawl a Belle Isle shelter book. Stuart Sivertson, now eighty, still returns each summer to the site of his family's commercial fishing camp on Washington Island.

Paddlers arrive with different goals. The 112-mile circumnavigation has been made in four days. To circumnavigate that quickly, however, requires long crossings. I am pokier than that; tracing shores close enough to feel each wave respond to the shallow bottom by steepening under my hull. I can't resist stopping to inspect an old fishing boat tugged onto the shore. Or to read names etched on hundred-year-old wooden grave markers, barely readable under gray-green lichen.

Observing the once worn Rock Harbor Lighthouse tower, now freshly whitewashed and gleaming against the dark forest, or making lunch on the Wright Island cabin porch, you'll soak in Isle Royale's history. Wooden walls, collapsing into dirt below, reminds us that the consequences of our lives will ripple forward for a time and fade.

Whether you are coming to bust miles, to relax and explore, or for a blend of both, you've waited long enough. Our lives are shorter than we think. This is your time to go.

The Isle Royale Archipelago

A billion years ago, lava flooded through cracks in the earth's mantle. Now waves break over lithified tongues of these ancient flows. Water glugs into cavities left by ancient magma gas bubbles. Twelve thousand years ago, glaciers scraped sediment from the valleys between basalt ridges. The resulting fjord shelters you from Lake Superior storms. You are paddling an environment forged by fire and ice.

Isle Royale's human history spans time from 4,500-year-old copper pits to a pedal sewing machine, visible through warped glass and lace curtains. From the frayed nets of a 1900s fishing camp, the graying hulls of wooden boats tucked along her shores, to heeled leather boots with rows of pearled buttons recovered from a luxury steamer shipwreck. This chapter is your introduction to Isle Royale geologic, natural, and human history.

Ancient Rock Shapes Our Journey

The heart of Isle Royale's geology is the Laurentian craton, the foundation of landscapes from Texas to the Arctic Ocean, from New Mexico to the Appalachian Mountains. Its past includes a marriage with Greenland and Scotland's Hebridean Terrane.

Portage Lake Volcanics

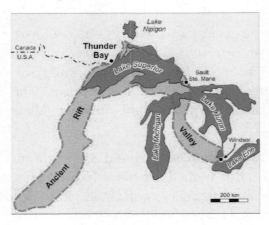

Ancient Rift Valley

About a billion years ago, in the Precambrian Period, melted rock floated toward the earth's surface from deep within the Laurentian mantle. Against the pressure of this rising magma, fissures opened along two legs, straddling a rift arc from what is now Kansas into Michigan. The heart of this arc would become the Lake Superior basin.

For 24 million years, lava spewed through the fissures, flooded thousands of square miles, and heaped another massive rock sheet onto the stack. Geologists have named this rock sequence the Portage Lake Volcanics.

Its center sank beneath the weight of this heavy rock stack. Its edges tilted upward. The northern edges formed Isle Royale. Southern edges became the Keweenaw Peninsula. Each ridge, island chain, and reef along Isle Royale's northeast-southwest axis are basalt from these lava flows. The tops of lava beds form Isle Royale's southeast-facing rock planes. Her northwest-facing cliffs are edges and bottoms of volcanic sheets.

Cooling lava encased gas bubbles with rock. Over eons, mineral-bearing water percolated through the voids and filled the smaller ones with amygdaloids and agates. The hexagonal columns on Edwards Island, on the trail from Rock Harbor to Mount Franklin, and west of Daisy Farm on the path to Mount Ojibway, mark places of rapid lava cooling.

Between eruptions, streams eroded the rock and carried gravel, sand, and mud to fill the sinking Lake Superior basin. Time and pressure solidified these sediments into Copper Harbor Conglomerate. Much of the Isle Royale shore from Fishermans Home Cove to Rainbow Cove, including Long Point, the Head, Rainbow, and Cumberland Points, are formed from Copper Harbor Conglomerate. Its eroded stone and gravel form beaches along Isle Royale's southwest shore.

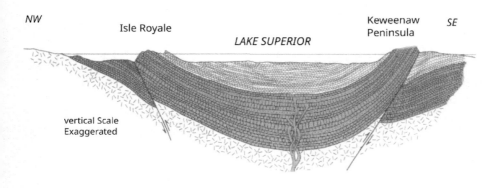

Lake Superior Basin Syncline, from Huber

Glaciation

The glaciers of a long string of ice ages carved Isle Royale's landscape. Her most recent sculptor, about twelve thousand years ago, was Wisconsin Glaciation. Ice sheets, hundreds of feet thick, pulverized softer sedimentary rock, carved out Lake Superior's basin, and chiseled the slender fingers of Isle Royale's fjords, marshes, and lakes. It etched long striations into resistant rock along Tobin and Rock Harbor's north shores, and at Moskey Basin Campground, Pickerel Cove, Lake Richie, and Siskiwit Lake.

West of Siskiwit Bay, the ice flow twisted and cut across the ridge and valley washboards. It mantled Isle Royale's older rock with glacial till. Ice eddies deposited ridged drumlins, two feet to two miles long, behind resistant rock.

As the climate warmed, the ice retreated in fits and starts. Ice tongues melted, abandoning recessional moraines, and jettisoning arc-shaped berms of sand, gravel, and fine glacial till. Moraines on Mount Desor's south side, for example, mark the recession of an ice lobe along the Little Siskiwit River basin.

Lake Superior's Ancestral Lakes

Each time glacial meltwater punched a new outlet from the Lake Superior basin, water levels changed abruptly. Each new water level change marked another in a series of lakes occupying the Lake Superior basin. From oldest to youngest, these lakes were Duluth, Washburn, Beaver Bay, Nipissing, Minong, and Houghton. Each new lake eroded cliffs, carved arches and built beaches along their shores.

Retreating ice formed the northeast lake margins. During the times of Lakes Duluth and Washburn, Isle Royale remained ice-covered. But Lake Beaver Bay ice retreated to uncover about ten miles of Isle Royale's western end. Since then, each lake has marked the Isle Royale landscape. West of

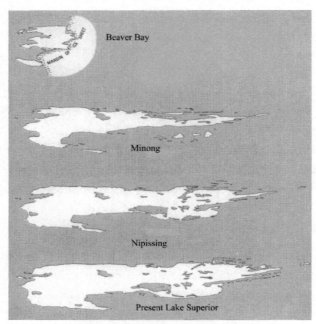

Lake Superior's Ancestral Lakes, from Huber

Siskiwit Bay, the Island Mine and Feldtmann Ridge Trails cross Lake Minong and Lake Nipissing beach gravel. They skirt their wave-cut cliffs. Lake Nipissing waves chiseled Amygdaloid Island's arch and Suzy's Cave on Rock Harbor.

Copper

Everywhere in the world, except on Isle Royale and the Keweenaw Peninsula, copper occurs only bound into minerals. The rare metallic copper found in these two locations migrated from hot rock deep in the Lake Superior syncline. It flowed into lava ridge and conglomerate bed cavities and fissures. Native copper on the Keweenaw Peninsula is the world's most valuable metallic copper deposit.

On Isle Royale, farther from the Lake Superior syncline, copper mineralization was too weak to form large lode deposits. Copper occurred in nodules and irregular fracture zones a few inches to feet wide. Copper masses of more than a ton, like one found at the Minong Mine, were rare.

Greenstones and Other Semiprecious Gems

Collecting any rock from Isle Royale National Park violates Park regulations.

Chlorastrolite means "green star stone" and its more common name is greenstone. Weathered from amygdules in Isle Royale lava flows, greenstones are scattered in Isle Royale fine beach gravel. Prehnite, another mineral precipitated into amygdules, also flecks fine Isle Royale beach gravel. Reflections of finely disseminated native copper in these stones produce colors from pale green to white or light to deep pink.

Quartz banded Isle Royale's volcanic cavities. Weather eroded the harder quartz's volcanic rock shell. Glaciers have strewn the resulting agates across Lake Superior beaches. Pink agates from the Amygdaloid Island flow are abundant. Long Island flow agates tend to be blue.

Natural History

Southwest winds drove waves against twenty feet of gravel on Amygdaloid Island's rocky tip. Twenty miles beyond 12 O'clock Point, streaks of cirrus clouds intersected the blue hills of Minnesota's North Shore. Only a white dot against the vast expanse of blue, probably a fishing boat, suggested another human presence.

This million-dollar view compensated for a simple lunch of rosemary crackers, Irish cheddar, and summer sausage. There was nothing ordinary, though, about the dark chocolate and pecan cinnamon bar. I licked its wrapper.

As I cut thin slices of sausage, I heard soft clicks. I slowly turned toward my right shoulder, where a dragonfly's three-inch wings framed its green upper lip and lower blue jaw. It wiggled the last bits of thin mosquito legs and the tips of miniature brown wings into its maw. Barely breathing, I studied a faceted brown eye which studied me.

Isle Royale's natural communities have been shaped by geology, by glaciation, and by the disturbances of fire, wind, and storms. Its many communities combine into three primary ecosystems: uplands; wetlands, lakes, and streams; and Lake Superior's shore.

Uplands

Where thin soils hold little moisture, Isle Royale's rippling ridges are home to plant communities that can withstand wind and lightning strikes. Lichens, creeping juniper, grasses, and blueberries find footing on south-sloping rock outcrops. Jack, white, and red pine twist their roots into fractures. Cedar, spruce, balsam fir, aspen, mountain ash, paper birch, Canada yew, and ferns cling to north-facing slopes. Thimbleberry thickets, bunchberry, bluebead-lily, sarsaparilla, club moss, and liverwort blanket the shaded forest floors.

Cladina rangiferina,
Reindeer Lichen

Isle Royale's southwestern end hosts deeper soil formed from glacial sediment. Maple and yellow birch find homes here. Sugar Mountain's name remembers Ojibwe sugar camps on its slopes.

Wetlands, Lakes, and Streams

Swamp forests, bogs, wetlands, and streams occupy Isle Royale's long valley fingers. Tag alder, black spruce, tamarack, white cedar, and ash grow in drier ground. Sphagnum moss, sedges, and skunk cabbage fringe the boardwalk trails.

Moose tracks gouge black swamp muck. Unless the moose have browsed them all, sedges, horsetails, milfoil, pondweed, and water lilies sprout from open water. Fireweed's magenta blooms commonly edge these marshes. The headwaters of Duncan Bay, Chippewa, Washington, and Tobin Harbors invite a paddling exploration of these gentle waters.

The Lake Superior Shore

Achillea millefolium
Yarrow on Blake Point

Lake Superior's shore is a kayaker's domain. Geology provides three distinct shore environments: north-facing cliffs; basaltic and conglomerate bedrock slopes and headlands; and gravel and cobble beaches.

Cliffs dominate the north shores of Isle Royale and its archipelago. Lichens, with a palette from orange to green to gray, grab toeholds on vertical rock, where the setting sunlight sets their striking colors ablaze. Harebells, grasses, and trees thread roots into cracks to take their one chance at life. Isle Royale's north shore, from John's Island to Blake Point, offers opportunities to kayak beside these vertical cliff communities. Smaller cliff stretches occur on the north shores of islands in Rock and Washington Harbors.

Mosses, lichens, shrubby cinquefoil, low-growing shrubs and wildflowers cling to the wave and ice-scrubbed rock of Isle Royale's gentler south-facing shores. Aquatic insects and chorus frogs inhabit bedrock splash pools. Butterworts and sundews supplement nitrogen, absent from the rock, by trapping and digesting insects in their sticky leaves. Look for these carnivorous plants along Blake Point's southwest shore, and in the Raspberry Island bogs.

Rainbow Cove, Attwood Beach, Blueberry Cove, and the east end of Belle Isle are examples of the rare gravel and cobble beaches that form where headlands break Lake Superior's energy. Alder, ninebark, wild rose, raspberries, and dewberries grow above the tumble-polished stones. Beach peas, identifiable by their pink flowers or edible green fruit, grow on Isle Royale's warmer, south-facing beaches.

Mammals

All Isle Royale life descended from those who arrived as we do, across Lake Superior. But lacking diesel-powered ferry transport, only about twenty out of the fifty mainland mammal species have crossed the icy water to establish a home on Isle Royale.

Except for the Norway rat, who probably stowed away on a boat, the crossing must've been an adventure. Bats of six distinct species certainly flew. River otters and beaver swam. Moose either swam or were brought by hunters from the mainland. Wolves crossed ice bridges that, before climate warming, connected Canada and Isle Royale every two or three winters. Caribou, foxes, lynx, and coyote likely made similar ice bridge crossings. But did squirrels, tiny deer mice, mink, marten, and ermine make a fourteen-mile run across open ice between mainland and Island woods? Or did they float on bits of wood?

Before moose arrived on Isle Royale in the early 1900s, Isle Royale's apex predator-prey relationship was caribou and coyote. For fifty years after their arrival, however, Isle Royale's coyote was no match and did little to keep moose populations in balance. Moose numbers boomed and busted with weather and food abundance.

But in the harsh winter of 1949, at least one breeding wolf pair crossed the ice bridge from Ontario. From those two wolves, the Isle Royale packs were born. Since then, wolf numbers have fluctuated between fifty in 1980, to a low of two in 2016.

Fox and wolves roam the human trail system. Scat glistens with the white hairs of their last meal. When wolves threaten moose calves, cows bring them into the safer human realm of campgrounds. Snowshoe hares nibble campground grasses. Red foxes patrol at twilight and dawn. Generations of foxes—in Daisy Farm they are all named Ransom—crave our salty footwear. Leave a boot to air on the shelter doorstep and you may find it missing in the morning.

Wolves are less commonly seen. Even researchers summer on Isle Royale without encountering one. But first-time Isle Royale visitors sometimes get lucky. If you are one of these, take a single breath to absorb this unique experience. Then make a loud noise and chase the wolf away. Their reluctance to interact with humans has allowed wolves to coexist with Isle Royale visitors for decades.

Birds

Redheaded mergansers cruise a rocky shore at sunset, sixteen chicks synchronously diving and popping back to the surface like corks. A solitary loon floats fifty feet from shore, mindless of the waves. Bald eagles perch on a tree skeleton, scanning the water for lunch.

Isle Royale birds respond to progressions of forest and wetland vegetation; to changes from the decimation of beaver populations and their resurgence; to fires set to clear vast swaths of vegetation and expose its surface copper. Common Isle Royale birds are sandhill cranes, great blue herons, downy woodpeckers, snow buntings, winter wrens, ovenbirds, and cormorants.

Creepy, Crawly, Slithery, and Biting Ones

Although not as teeming as on the warmer Boundary Water Canoe Area or Lake Huron waters, mosquitoes on Isle Royale are a thing. Their numbers vary between years and seasons. They tend to be most ferocious in June and near swamps and bogs. Black flies and deerflies can be annoying, particularly in June. Be prepared for the occasional red, itchy welt of a no-see-um. There are leeches in Isle Royale's interior lakes and Lake Superior's warm coves.

Isle Royale hosts only one tick. While the winter tick plagues moose--80,000 on a moose drink gallons of their blood--they are completely uninterested in humans.

Human History

Introduction

An Isle Royale encounter often begins with "How often have you come?" Five and ten times are common answers. Stuart Sivertson, eighty-one years old the summer we met, has come nearly every year since he was nine. Although a few intrepid souls have wintered over, Isle Royale has primarily been a place for summer visits. Sojourners have arrived over millennia to wet lines and feast on her fat fish. To pick berries, sugar maples, and mine copper. To linger on a pea gravel beach as the sun sinks behind a ridge, and the sky deepens into a long twilight pool.

Isle Royale holds memories and relics. Modernity has not erased net-drying reels anchored into rock-filled barrels, mine shafts, or a whitewashed lighthouse tower. Time slows. Distractions are fewer.

Ojibwe History

When the last ice sheet receded ten thousand years ago, ancestors of the Lake Superior Chippewa Grand Portage Band already inhabited the Upper Great Lakes. Seen from their tribal lands, Isle Royale stretches a thin dark band across Lake Superior's horizon. In Anishinaabemowin, Isle Royale is called Minong. One of Minong's many translations is "the good place."

Minong threads the fabric of Lake Superior Chippewa and Ojibwe heritage. Generations have come to hunt caribou and beaver. They sugared maple trees in late winter and gathered summer's sweet blueberries. They fished Minong's reefs with spears, hooks, and gill nets, and cured their catch by drying and smoking. For over 4,500 years, Ojibwe dug pits and pounded raw copper from bedrock veins. They traded knives, points, and ornaments, cold-hammered from Minong copper, across the continent.

Along with their practical relationships with the Island, Minong threads through the Ojibwe understanding of the sacred. A powerful manitou, the great under-water wildcat, Mishipeshu, guards access to Minong's precious copper. Hear their roar in storms. Ojibwe sprinkle tobacco on bare rock beneath Manido Gizhigans, the Little Cedar Spirit Tree, to ensure a safe crossing of fourteen miles of Lake Superior's unsheltered water.

The United States claimed Isle Royale from the Ojibwe in the 1842 Treaty of La Pointe. European settlers supplanted traditional Isle Royale activities with commercial copper mining and fishing. They founded their Isle Royale enterprises, however, on Ojibwe knowledge, skills, and labor. Ojibwe worked mines and cruised timber. They trapped and fished for the American Fur Company. They guided and cooked for resort visitors. They staffed fire-fighting teams that fought Isle Royale fires in 1936 and 1948.

Grand Portage Band tribal members continue their relationship with Minong. They fish her waters and return to gather berries and nourish their historical and spiritual traditions. In 2019, Isle Royale was designated a Minong Traditional Cultural Property, recognizing the relationship between Minong and the Grand Portage Band of Lake Superior Chippewa.

Copper Mining

Ojibwe crossed Lake Superior in small boats to mine Isle Royale copper at least 4,500 years ago. They heated and quenched rock and stone hammered the metal from exposed veins.

After the 1842 treaty, however, commercial operations supplanted traditional mining. Readily available venture capital spurred an unrealistic belief in easy fortunes. Companies with U.S.-issued permits incorporated in New York, Vermont, Ohio, Michigan, and Illinois to establish Isle Royale mines.

The newly formed companies cruised Isle Royale shores, scanning for copper veins. They burned forests to expose and examine bedrock. They constructed settlements at Ransom (now Daisy Farm), Windigo, Siskiwit Bay, and Snug and Todd Harbors. Mining families planted gardens in thin soil for potatoes, peas, lettuce, and radishes to supplement tea and beef shipped from the mainland. Most miners evacuated each winter, leaving only skeleton crews.

Isle Royale's isolation and harsh winters made mining difficult and expensive. The Isle Royale copper boom was short-lived, and the last mine closed in 1855.

Commercial Fishing

"Fishing wasn't always profitable, but it was always interesting."

–Stan Sivertson, in A Good Boat Speaks for Itself.

A southwest wind blew twelve knots across a thirty-mile fetch. With an eye toward the bumpy water, I scanned the thick woods of Johns Island's shore for a glimpse of its old cabin, then turned south. Ten minutes later, I pulled into the well-protected harbor between Washington and Barnum Islands. A Finnish, Swedish, and Norwegian flag each flapped from a pole above three docks. The closest dock house, a long, gray building with freshly milled two-by-fours stacked on its deck, bore a grayed plank etched with the name of Isle Royale fishing royalty: Sivertson. A lanky, gray-haired man in comfortably faded jeans and a flannel shirt greeted me from the adjacent shore.

"Would you like to land and visit? I can give you a tour."

The original Isle Royale fishers were people of the Lake Superior Chippewa and Ojibwe bands. European immigrant fishing began when the American Fur Company established a station on Belle Isle in July 1837.

Isle Royale's commercial fishing families have been primarily Scandinavian immigrants. Fishing Scandinavia's chilly water prepared them for the hardships of Lake Superior. When fishing families arrived in mid-April, their homes were often still locked behind shore ice. They worked seven days a week, taking off only the Fourth of July, until November storms and the threat of freeze-up drove them back to the mainland.

Transporting materials from the mainland was expensive. Fishing family homes were small; often built from reused mine lumber, salvaged shipwrecks, and logs gleaned from those lost from timber rafts. The Sivertson fish house, for example, was a reclaimed Civilian Conservation Corps building hauled to Washington Island from Windigo.

Early commercial fishing boats were Mackinaws. Constructed of oak boards, with flat bottoms, blunt ends, a rudder, and mast, they could be either sailed or rowed. Forty-foot schooners, the *William Brewster* and the *Siskawit,* transported fish to market in the early 1900s.

Edisen Fishery Net House

In 1926, the State of Michigan required Lake Superior commercial fishers to be licensed. In the 1940s, the Atlantic sea lamprey population exploded, decimating 90 percent of Lake Superior's profitable lake trout. By 1966, only eight Isle Royale commercial fishers were registered, compared to seventy-five registered families in the 1920s. Isle Royale's last commercial fisher, Stanley Sivertson, died in 1994 at eighty.

Shipwrecks and Lighthouses

Isle Royale straddles Lake Superior's major shipping lanes. November's gales, fog and ice have ringed her with ten major shipwrecks. The shipwrecks and Lake Superior commercial mining interests inspired construction of four Isle Royale lighthouses—Passage Island, Rock of Ages,

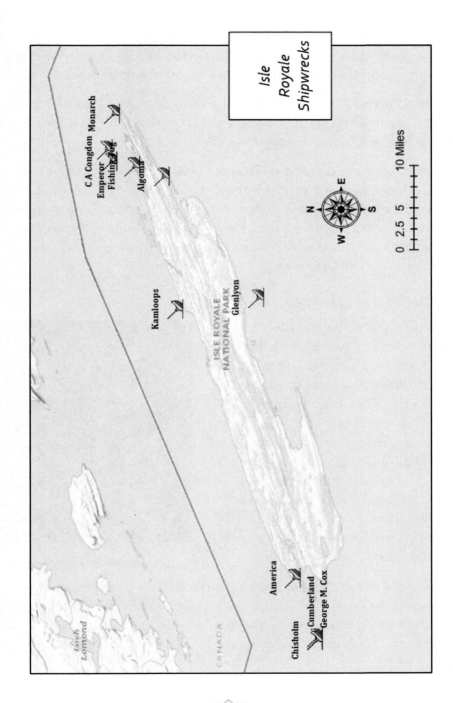

Isle Royale Shipwrecks

Loch Lomond

CANADA

C A Congdon Monarch
Emperor
Fishing Tug
Algoma

Kamloops

Glenlyon

ISLE ROYALE
NATIONAL PARK

America
Chisholm
Cumberland
George M. Cox

N E
W   S

0   2.5   5   10 Miles

Isle Royale, and Rock Harbor. Before their lights were automated, lightkeepers and their families tended the lights and rescued shipwreck survivors from the end of April until just before ice-up in mid-November. The long season spanned many days of fog and stormy weather.

Few kayakers make the twelve-mile round-trip journey to Passage Island or even the five-mile paddle to Rock of Ages Lighthouse. But the Rock Harbor and Isle Royale Lighthouses are accessible.

While ice has gouged and dispersed the hulls of wooden vessels, most of the metal steamers lie virtually intact. Lake Superior's cold water has preserved oaken ribs, massive anchors, sheeted bunks, and mattresses. Leather boots lie as they have since the moments of disaster. Kayakers along Isle Royale shores encounter buoys marking three wrecks: the *Monarch*, the *Algoma*, and the *America*.

Passage Island Lighthouse

Silver deposits on Silver Islet, Ontario increased the number of ships threading the six-mile-wide channel between Isle Royale's Blake Point and Passage Island. In 1875 the US Congress appropriated $18,000 to construct the Passage Island lighthouse. An oil-burning wick lamp beamed through a fixed red fourth order lens. A ten-inch steam-powered fog whistle replaced the original mechanical fog bell in 1884. On September 24, 1897, a flashing white light replaced the original fixed red light.

Passage Island Lighthouse

Near the end of the 1883 navigation season, Passage Island lightkeeper W. Dermant motored to Port Arthur for supplies. While he was there, Lake Superior froze unexpectedly, stranding his wife and three children until spring thaw. They survived the winter by fishing and hunting snowshoe hares.

There are no moose on Passage Island. Unbrowsed vegetation creates a unique island ecosystem that is worth a visit. There is no camping allowed, however, on Passage Island. Lack of an overnight option, and the 12-mile round trip crossing open water, suggest booking a water taxi from Rock Harbor Marina for your Passage Island trip.

Rock of Ages Lighthouse

The Rock of Ages reef lies two and a half miles southwest of Washington Island, straddling an active shipping route between Duluth and Thunder Bay. The wreck of three large ships, the *Cumberland* in 1877, the *Henry Chisholm* in 1898, and the *George M Cox* in 1933 on its shallow rock inspired construction of the Rock of Ages Lighthouse.

Rock of Ages Lighthouse

A fifty-foot steel crib anchors a 117-foot cylinder of steel, concrete, and brick to the slender basalt outcrop. Two basement levels housed water tanks. A boiler blasted steam heat into the tower. An office occupied the third level, staff sleeping quarters the fourth and fifth levels, and a watch room was installed on the sixth level. Plaster and wood baseboard, door and window trim finished its interior walls. Closets and cabinets fitted below the stairwells.

The Rock of Ages' fixed red light was lit on October 11, 1908. A year later, a second order Fresnel lens replaced the original light. The nine-foot lens, now on display in the Windigo Visitor Center, twirled on a mercury puddle atop a cast-iron pedestal. The most powerful of the Great Lake beacons, it was visible on a clear night across twenty-nine miles.

A four-member crew staffed the light until 1977. Today, solar energy powers the automated light.

On the night of May 27, 1933, 127 passengers and the crew from the wrecked *George M. Cox*, arrived at the Rock of Ages Lighthouse for shelter. With insufficient room inside for everyone, crew and passengers took turns huddling outside on the bare rock and warming themselves inside the tower.

Summer Visitors

"On a map of Isle Royale, it seems always to be 1935, with names like Gale Island, Barnum Island, Edwards Island, Davidson Island, and Merritt Lane. Many of the families still visit the islands that bear their names, adding to the illusion that seventy years have not actually passed since the last regattas in Tobin Harbor."-David Newland, Isle Royale National Park Staff.

By 1890, copper companies had abandoned hope of mining profits from Isle Royale's isolated and harsh environment. But on the mainland, lumber, railroads, and iron mining boomed. The Sault Saint Marie Canal connected Lake Superior to the rest of the Great Lakes and the Atlantic Ocean. In 1869, Duluth was the fastest growing city in the country. Dr. Thomas Foster, the founder of its first newspaper, dubbed Duluth the "Zenith City of the Unsalted Seas." By the early 1900s, the Duluth port was the busiest in the United States, surpassing even New York City's gross tonnage.

As wealth fueled leisure, city residents grew hungry to escape crowded and unsanitary urban life. So Isle Royale mining companies conjured a new moneymaking dream: tourism. Along with fish and mining settlement supplies, steamers transported urban refugees to enjoy Isle Royale's cool summer temperatures, fishing, and what was described as the "strenuous life."

In 1901, an excursion from Duluth to Washington Harbor cost $5 round trip. Visitors camped or rented fishing camp accommodations. John F. Johns rented his Barnum Island cottage. Holger Johnson welcomed visitors into the Chippewa Harbor fish camp. John Linklater hosted tourists on Birch Island.

The Isle Royale Land Corporation surveyed a town site close to the Ransom Mine, planning hotels, bathhouses, dance halls, toboggan slides, and summer theaters. Captain Singer built a resort with a hotel and cottage accommodations on Washington Island. Duluthians purchased the twenty-room Wendigo Company headquarters at the head of Washington Harbor for their exclusive private club. In 1901, Kneut Knuetson established Park Place resort at the present Rock Harbor Lodge location.

Other resorts developed near the head of Tobin Harbor, Davidson Island, and Belle Isle. In 1914, buyers snapped up Tobin Harbor islands for summer cottages. Summer cottage families arrived each year at the end of school and stayed until September. They caught fish, chopped wood, collected water, and repaired their homes. Moose-watching and photography were part of Isle Royale leisure life. While self-sufficiency had been a requirement for commercial fishing families, summer cottagers relied on the fishers to fix motorboats, repair buildings, and supply fish for dinner.

Creating a National Park

The idea of an Isle Royale National Park was conceived in a decade dubbed the "Roaring Twenties." World War I was over. Economies boomed. Women shortened their skirts and bobbed their hair. Telephones, motion pictures, radio, and electricity penetrated American homes. Babe Ruth hit home runs out of the ballpark.

That was the decade in which Albert Stoll, Jr., the Detroit News conservation editor, began a campaign to protect Isle Royale. He wrote that, in contrast to the mainland's clear-cut forests, Isle Royale's ridges were *"never molested by the lumberman's ax"* and its vertical basalt, pounded by Lake Superior waves, seemed to Stoll to be *"practically the only bit of unspoiled nature east of the Mississippi River."*

As Americans hurled toward modernity, Stoll's writing resonated with a national longing to preserve our relationship with wilderness. Millions of people, recently transplanted from farms into cities, resonated with Stoll's description of nature as a clean, invigorating place for "manly" activities.

They hungered for a refuge from what seemed to them to be the amoral, easy life of urban centers; places that threatened, in their minds, to "feminize" America's youth.

Isle Royale's summer visitors swung golf clubs, tugged fish from the lakes, and played rummy on their porches. But Island Copper Company sale of 66,500 acres of western Isle Royale for paper pulp outraged summer cottagers. The rumble of clear-cutting, smoky fires, and decimated wildlife would defile their summer idylls.

In August 1922, while timber prospectors cruised their Island, summer residents organized. They wrote a letter to John Baird, director of Michigan's Department of Conservation, requesting he designate Isle Royale a Timber and Game Preserve. A Minneapolis business owner and cottager, Frank Warren, wrote articles calling for a Federal Forest and Wildlife Preserve. Their urgent pleas, however, elicited no response.

But the power of public sentiment was stirring. Prominent Midwest journalists joined Stoll's call to protect Isle Royale. Visions coalesced around Isle Royale as a national park. Even the Island Copper Company supported park designation, as long as they retained their mineral rights.

Finally, only the National Park Service itself was not on board. Previous national parks had been carved from federally owned land. Buying out Isle Royale's private landowners would be expensive. But in January 1924, National Park Director Mather asked the Detroit News to arrange an Isle Royale trip for himself and Interior Secretary Hubert Work. After his visit, Mather declared that Isle Royale "would make the finest water and trail park that I can think of."

National Park Service Staff Visit Isle Royale in 1924

In August 1935, President Roosevelt authorized $70,000 to purchase private Isle Royale property. One key question remained: what to do with Isle Royale's fishing and summer cottage families? The United States Army forcibly removed Indigenous communities from Yellowstone National Park, establishing a precedent to exclude private national park inhabitation.

But removing Indigenous and poor white communities was easier than displacing families with financial and political clout. In 1932, Congress approved leases for adults who had lived on Isle Royale. Summer cottagers glommed onto the process for residents and negotiated leases that allowed themselves and their children to continue occupying their summer homes within park boundaries.

The Park Service also offered special use permits to commercial fishing families, even if they did not own their fishing camps. On April 3, 1940, the National Park Service acquired the last private Isle Royale acreage. Thirty families opted for life leases, and most fishers remained. A dedication ceremony on Mott Island in 1946 established Isle Royale National Park.

A National Park for Everyone

We sat on the aluminum storage lifejacket bin across Voyager II's foredeck. A stranger's body next to mine deflected a chilly wind. Opaque blue nails tipped each of his long, bronzed fingers.

"Nice nails."

Over the next hour of monotonous Lake Superior journey, we compared routes. He described a memorable pasta dinner with his three traveling companions. Not until we rounded Grand Portage Island and Hat Marina came into view, did he offer "Actually, this trip was a bachelor party for me and my boyfriend. We are getting married. We all painted our fingernails when we arrived on the Island. Sometimes, chatting with people I didn't know, I wondered if I should try to hide them."

While many Isle Royale visitors, from two to eighty-two, are arriving for the first-time, Isle Royale is the most revisited US National Park. Isle Royale is, however, something of a Midwestern secret; relatively unknown in the rest of the country. Isle Royale is, theoretically, accessible to anyone. But it's mostly the Island's white colonizer history that's celebrated in books and museums, in the relics of resorts and fishing camps. Within the National Park, Isle Royale's history before European colonization is invisible. This reality shapes everyone's experience. It limits who feels welcome.

Get Set

Answering the Call

As the crew handed down our last boat into four waiting arms, I noticed a single kayak remained. Lowering seventeen feet of kayak from the Voyager II's top deck and then juggling it for a twenty-yard carry is a difficult solo act. When we'd set our boat in the grass, I ran back to help.

His thirty-something face sported a week's whiskers. Muscular, bronzed calves and thighs were visible below his board shorts. He walked the front of his kayak toward his car and the crew lowered its stern into my raised hands.

It was just fifty steps during which he described his seven-day Isle Royale circumnavigation. But I was gobsmacked by the idea of kayaking Isle Royale solo. In the intervening year, I replaced my twenty-eight-year-old stove and fifteen-year-old tent. I baked and bagged granola, dehydrated black beans, packed masa, and Celtic sea salt.

As a gear pile waxed and waned in a corner of my dining room, I considered what I needed versus what I'd have room for. I warned clients, friends, and kiddos that I'd be unreachable for twenty-one days. My stomach churned. I wondered whether a long solo journey was crazy. But crazy or not, I was going.

You've heard adventure's call and your heart has said "yes!" But safely paddling Lake Superior's frigid and sometimes stormy water requires adequate equipment, skills, and knowledge of Lake Superior conditions. Myriad decisions lie between this moment and your first Isle Royale paddle stroke. It's time to begin the nitty-gritty of planning. When will you go? With whom? What route will you take? What do you need? This chapter will help you navigate all that.

Cautions and Considerations

Communication

Kayaking Isle Royale was better before cell service nicked its shores. Your boss, friends, and family could write you a letter. But other than that, you were out of reach.

Now, depending on your cell phone carrier, you might pick up messages or even a phone call from the Malone Bay dock, the west end of Washington Harbor, along Isle Royale's north shore, or even a ridge. Visitor Centers in Rock Harbor and Windigo can accommodate emergency satellite calls. In some years it has also been possible to purchase private satellite phone service from the concession stores. You'll be charged for each minute.

Hypothermia

Lake Superior's summer water temperatures are unpredictable, ranging from the 40s to the 60s. In some places and seasons, you will enjoy a brisk swim. Other times and places, the water is bone-aching cold and even a short time submerged is dangerous. Cold hands may not be able to flip a boat, grip a paddle, or grasp a deck line.   In less than five minutes, it's possible to lose the ability to make coordinated hand and finger movements necessary for a rescue. The initial shock of an icy plunge can produce disorientation or cardiac arrest. You may inhale water in an involuntary gasp for breath.

Launch only in conditions you can confidently paddle. Always wear your life jacket and fasten your spray skirt. A dry suit or 5 mm wet suit is ideal. If you found yourself in frigid water with neither an immersion garment nor your boat, your outlook would be grim indeed.

Wear synthetic thermal, fleece, or wool base layers, top and bottom. Cotton or nylon clothing isn't warm enough.   Layer up *before* making a crossing. You might feel comfortable near shore, but cold as you paddle onto the open lake. Keep a dry top, splash jacket, or storm cag handy. When you land, add layers before you get chilled. It is easier to stay warm than to get warm.

Eat well and hydrate before setting out and after a long day. You'll also sleep more comfortably if you are well fed.

Know hypothermia's warning signs:

- Feeling cold
- Impaired mental ability
- Erratic paddling and inability to maintain course
- Blurred vision
- Slurred speech
- Lack of coordination
- Uncontrollable shivering
- Despondency
- Ashen face and hands

Keep watch for these symptoms in your team. Let your companions know if you recognize any of these symptoms in yourself. Anyone who expresses hopelessness or despondency should be observed for additional warning signs.

Address hypothermia symptoms immediately. Don't wait! Medical help should be sought for anyone with altered mental ability, sleepiness, unconsciousness, or slowed, irregular breathing or heartbeat. Offer anyone who is shivering sugary or high-calorie beverages and food to sustain their energy. If they are able, get them moving. Help them change into dry clothing and shelter them from wind. Apply warm packs or another body to armpits, groin, neck, and trunk, but *not* to arms or legs, which would draw blood from vital core organs.

Emergencies

Broken bones, sprains, and wounds are serious emergencies in Isle Royale's isolated environment. Bring a first aid kit and be prepared to handle first aid situations. Read a first aid book or, better yet, take wilderness first aid or wilderness first-responder training.

Assume that, in an emergency, you will have no cell phone service. US Coast Guard, park rangers, motor and sailboats monitor VHF Channel 16, but communication is limited to line-of-sight. Help might not reach an injured person for hours or even days. If you've brought an emergency personal location beacon, use it only to summon an urgent evacuation.

If an injured person is near shore, a park boat can transport them to first aid. Transport from interior trails, however, requires a park litter. In a life-threatening emergency, weather might allow helicopter transport from Windigo, Rock Harbor, or Mott Island. The closest hospital is in Thunder Bay, Ontario, Canada.

Your group will leave an itinerary with park staff. You are not obligated to follow that itinerary, but if you fail to arrive for your schedule ferry departure, park staff will initiate a search based on their available information.

Dangers and Annoyances

Isle Royale has no bears or poisonous snakes. The most potentially dangerous animals on the Island are moose. Females protect their young. Bull moose may be aggressive during their fall rut. Give any moose you encounter a wide berth. Step behind a tree and wait for them to pass. Wolves are rarely seen. Should you encounter a wolf, keep your distance, and end your encounter quickly by making loud noises. Shout. Clap your hands. Report wolf sightings to a ranger.

Toxic cyanobacteria algae blooms have been reported at Intermediate and Chickenbone Lakes, Lake Richie, and Lake Livermore. These algae-released toxins are **not** removed by filtering, boiling, or disinfection. Do not use water from these lakes. Do not swim, fish, or drink from any water with a cloudy blue cast or what looks like "pea soup."

Mosquitoes and black flies are prevalent in June and early July. On wet summers, they will extend into August. Bring repellent, netting, or barrier clothing. If allergic to bee or wasp stings, bring an epinephrine kit.

Rocks at the water's edge can be slippery, making loading, launching, and landing treacherous. Wear water shoes with sticky soles. Zebra mussels have also been reported on Isle Royale. Protect your hands and feet from their sharp, cutting shells.

Poison ivy and poison oak are rare on Isle Royale, but you'll save yourself a world of trouble by learning to identify and avoid them. If you touch their leaves, stems, or roots, wash your skin as quickly as possible, ideally within thirty minutes of exposure. Tecnu deactivates the rash-causing urushiol oil. Warm soapy water is the next best option.

Timbers and stopes of Isle Royale copper mines are rotted, and their interiors are unsafe. Some shafts are unmarked and hidden by vegetation. Never enter an excavation and be careful around their edges. National Park regulations protect every structure and all artifacts. Photograph and enjoy them, but do not disturb them.

Thunderstorms and Seiches

Thunderstorms occur on Isle Royale from May through September, bringing intense rain, fierce wind, lightning, and hail. Monitor those bruised-blue clouds. Head to shore at the first flash and wait at least thirty minutes after the last rumble before launching. Shun tall trees, hilltops, and cliffs. The safest position from a lightning strike is crouched with your feet close together on an insulated sleeping pad or life jacket. If you are in a group, your chances of survival are better if you spread out.

Lake Superior has no tidal surges. Wind and air pressure fluctuations, however, produce seiches. The unexpected water level change has swept more than one Isle Royale kayak from what seemed like a safe berth. Before settling into your camp, nestle your boat above the beach and secure it to a tree, rock, or alder branch. Do not camp beneath tall trees or dead branches. Secure your tarp and stake your tent for wind.

Staying Healthy and Preventing Paddling Injuries

Overstressed bodies react with pain and sometimes chronic damage. Blisters, muscle aches, and strains make a trip less pleasurable. Hand position is critical to prevent wrist pain. The line from your elbow to knuckles should be straight. An extended wrist, knuckles bent back toward the forearm, is an invitation to injury. The general opinion seems to be that feathering a paddle about fifteen degrees creates an optimal wrist position. My wrists, however, prefer unfeathered blades. Experiment to find what's best for your body. Hands should be shoulder-width apart and centered— mark your paddle shaft with waterproof tape to keep your hands well positioned.

Hold your paddle shaft with a light grip to prevent blisters. Practice stretching fingers wide on your pushing hand to balance the contraction effort of gripping muscles.

Keep your spine lifted with a natural curve and lift your solar plexus to prevent lower back soreness. Allow your shoulders to drop and lightly contract the muscles between the shoulder blades to protect your shoulders. Lengthen the back of your neck to prevent cramps. The elbow moves behind the waist to rudder, but not for the repetitive forward stroke. Recover your paddle blade at your hip.

Stretching all four fingers and thumb against a rubber band engages muscles to counter those used to grip the paddle and can relieve forearm pain. Finger resistance bands, with loops for each finger and the thumb, work even better than a rubber band. Keep them on your desk and use them during phone calls.

Strength training to target glutes, chest, back, biceps, triceps, lunges, and shoulders is invaluable. Pilates will improve the core strength necessary for a strong, efficient stroke. Paddling backward balances muscles that drive your forward stroke and also develops a vital kayaking skill. Warm-up before and cool down after hard paddling. Rolling over a foam cylinder or massage ball before and after paddling will speed recovery and improve flexibility.

Dehydration rapidly depletes your energy and makes you vulnerable to hypothermia, heat exhaustion, and stroke. Drink water before and while paddling. Add electrolytes to avoid water intoxication. If, after several paddling hours, you don't feel hungry, drink water with electrolytes.

Paddling Companions

Like Frodo setting out to toss the Ring into the Cracks of Mount Doom, your first key decision will be traveling companions. Your answer may be clear. A partner or a longtime paddling buddy. Maybe you'll set off on a family adventure that will challenge each of you individually and change who you are as a family. A few of us make the journey alone. This section offers pointers for group trips, trips with children, and going solo.

Groups

Six of us were preparing to kayak Isle Royale. We had spent a Sunday morning at Lake Travis, crossing motorboat wakes and dipping into Sandy Creek Cove. In deep water beneath limestone cliffs, we tipped our boats and swam, then turned them upright and stabilized them for each other to reenter.

One of us had driven to another launch on a different lake. They'd also missed previous group training paddles. Now we sat in my living room drinking cold hibiscus tea.

"I'm not sure I should go. Everyone but you and me is part of a couple. Are you going to be my buddy?"

I wasn't available for that, but I encouraged them to go. I shouldn't have. Years later, the wounds are not completely healed.

A group of paddlers has collective experience upon which to assess risks and make go/no-go decisions. In the event of an injury, someone can render first aid while someone else goes for help. When equipment fails, another group member might have the needed item.

A group will also share Isle Royale's magic. Golden moonbeams rippling across black water. The sense of accomplishment after a tough run. Laughter over dinner. Motivation to slip from a warm bag for a dawn launch. Shared memories are more durable.

Isle Royale National Park allows up to six people to occupy a single campsite or shelter. Groups of seven to ten make advanced reservations and camp in designated group sites. Groups larger than ten must split into two parties and travel on separate itineraries.

There are things you'll want to know about every group member. What is their paddling experience? How often do they get in their boat? How long is their typical trip? When did they last paddle? Do they have other wilderness camping experience? Do they enjoy long paddling days, or are afternoons on a sunny beach more of a priority? Is food simply fuel, or does a well-executed meal make their journey?

Each paddler should know how fast they paddle a loaded boat under various wind conditions. You'll also want to note the range of conditions they've experienced. Have they paddled against a fifteen-knot wind? Have they paddled two-foot waves? Landed in surf? Practiced self-rescues and assisted rescues? Before you head for the ferry, get on the water together and practice solo and assisted rescues.

Does anyone have medical conditions that might affect their ability to complete a trip? Have each paddler tuck a laminated card with health insurance and emergency contact information into a pocket of their life jacket so that crucial information will be handy in the stress of an emergency.

If you initiated the trip, you will automatically have some leadership responsibilities. But shared decision-making can quickly invest everyone. Let children help to plan menus.

Children

Storms had bound us in Rock Harbor. But the third morning dawned with light winds and calm seas. David and I hauled two kayaks to the dock and lugged gear from our shelter. We stuffed a tent and sleeping bags into triangular pouches shaped to fit our kayak's bow and stern. We crammed granola bars, cheese, and bags of pasta into huge rubber dry bags. Eamon and Geneva, just two and six, trotted beside us as we lugged everything to the Rock Harbor Marina docks.

Eager to get on the water, I scoffed at David's suggestion that we strap the kids into life jackets. Of course they would wear them on the water. But we were still on the dock!

Ker-splash! It was moments later when I turned from packing to see David sprawled across the concrete dock, one arm straining over its lip toward the loop on Geneva's yellow life jacket. Park rangers and ferry passengers lined the metal rail to watch as he hauled a startled, dripping two-year-old into his arms. But for her life jacket, they'd surely have taken that baby into the care of more responsible parents!

Kid Fun!

When kayaking with children, fun is a priority. Sift for greenstones on a sunny beach. Spend rainy afternoons snuggled under sleeping bags, reading aloud Ojibwe myths of manitous and wendigos. Cook pancakes with fresh thimbleberries and maple syrup. Plan layover days. Paddle unloaded boats.

Dance a line between overprotection and inattention. Let them scrape a knee, plunge from the end of a dock, scramble across slick rock. Plan to move on their schedule, with short paddles in calm conditions. On a beach, a stream, or a rock island a few feet from shore, they will travel places we've lost our capacity to visit. Soften our intrusive adult gaze. Give them space.

With no grocery store, no walls or roof, no blanketed mattress, even young children intuit how our choices impact comfort and survival. Sensing the raw vulnerability of Lake Superior's frigid water, they apprehend the importance of, literally, not rocking the boat. Include them in camp chores: filtering water, hauling gear, gathering berries, and helping with simple parts of meal preparation. Encourage a sense of their power in this wilderness environment.

They will, even in summer, need fleece jackets and pants to layer with synthetic thermal underwear and plenty of granola bars, dried apple slices, and almonds. Mix Tang with hot water for a cool day treat. A tent set up inside the shelter makes rainy afternoons or chilly nights snug.

Children from about age eleven can paddle an appropriately sized individual kayak. They'll need a lightweight, short paddle and a spray skirt. Their clothing should be suitable for a capsize. Make sure children (and everyone else) wear their life jackets whenever they are in a boat. Include them in wet-exit and assisted rescue practice.

Going Solo

"Those who truly have the solo kayaking inclination will not be stopped by anything I could say and do not stand in need of my blessing."

–John Dowd, in Sea Kayaking; a Manual for Long-Distance Touring

The sense of safety in a group can be deceptive. It is easy to get separated in wind and waves, the conditions in which we are most likely to capsize. A false sense of safety might compel us to launch into conditions that, if we were paddling solo, we'd take a pass on.

I am one for whom the siren call of solo kayaking will not be quelled either by the admonitions of others or by my own fear. Within the quiet aloneness, pitching a tarp or loading my boat becomes mindfulness practice. Against the consequences of spilled fuel, lighting my stove and shutting it down becomes ritual. Paddling solo magnifies my sense of vulnerability. Presence becomes a survival strategy. If kayaking solo is your jam, here are tips.

Avoid rock gardening. The consequence of riding swells squeezed by rock could be a busted hull on a lonely shore. The trouble you'd make for yourself and others is not worth the risk.

Develop your skills. Practice bracing and rolling in varying wind and wave conditions. You need more than one self-rescue method, and they need to be bombproof in any conditions you choose to paddle.

The risk of being separated from your boat on the water is highest when winds could push it beyond your reach. Prioritize and practice continuous solid contact with your boat in your rescues.

Dress for immersion in either a dry suit or a suitably thick wet suit.

Stay within conditions you can confidently paddle. Stay nourished. Food and water stave off hypothermia. Stop before you are exhausted. Listen to weather forecasts each morning and evening, and before embarking on committed reaches.

Be mindful of launching and landing your expedition-weight boat. Arrange driftwood into a beach ramp to protect your boat hull. Keep an emergency bag with essentials at hand.

Know your route before you launch. Identify potential bailout points: beaches, coves, and harbors. As you paddle, scan the shore. Could you land if you need to? Is there a suitable place for a camp?

Tether your kayak to shore if you leave it, even if only for a moment. Lake Superior's seiches have floated more than one shallowly beached boat.

Pets

A dog brought to Isle Royale in the 1980s introduced canine parvovirus, decimating its wolf population. Pets are strictly prohibited on Isle Royale or within its jurisdictional water, extending 4.5 miles from the Island's shore.

How Long?

Geneva, Ava, and I arrived at West Caribou Island in the early afternoon. We set up camp and spent the rest of the day sunning and swimming from the island's back beach. The girls, with a rapidly diminishing bag of dried apple slices between them, dangled slender, twelve-year-old legs over the basalt cliff.

It was much later when two men and two teenaged boys pulled kayaks onto the grass above the dock. They stripped out of life jackets and spray skirts, talking excitedly of how they'd paddled thirty miles that day on a following sea.

Paddling Isle Royale, our nervous system disconnects from the incessant staccato of cell phone rings and emails filling inboxes. We synchronize instead with the pulse of sunrise and twilight, the throb of a loon's call, rhythms of beach surf and aspen quiver. Carve out as many days for your journey as you can. Spoil yourself for your everyday life.

When?

Isle Royale National Park opens to visitors in mid-April and closes in November. The first ferry crossing, however, isn't until mid-May and the last ferry return is in early October.

Cypripedium acaule, Moccasin Flower

Between the first and last ferries, each season affords its own reasons for an Isle Royale paddle. June offers lady's slipper orchids' tender pink or yellow, forest floors carpeted with Canada dogwood, and velvety-white thimbleberry flowers as big as silver dollars. Strawberries and early blueberries ripen along sun strewn trails. In late June through early July, predawn illumination begins around 4:30 am. Evening twilight persists until after 10 pm. You might never see a dark sky.

Mosquitoes and deer flies are in full force in early summer. June weather can be stormy. Fishing families celebrated the arrival of settled weather with an island-wide July 4th picnic. Mid-July through mid-August sun heats beach stones while Lake Superior chills lake breezes. This season is also the most popular time for park visitors. Backpackers and motorboats will crowd campsites by early afternoon.

By Labor Day, summer crowds melt back to the mainland. Weather can be cooler and rainier. September storms may interrupt ferry schedules and pin small boats in harbors. Aspen leaves turn golden. Ripe thimbleberries, raspberries, blueberries, and apples on ancient trees in the remnants of Ransom Mine and Chippewa Harbor orchards are good reasons for a September Isle Royale journey.

Which Journey?

The sections below introduce three journeys, with enough information to choose the one best for your group's interests, time, and skills. The last sections of this book provide detailed information for each of the journeys.

The Rock Harbor Gateway Journey

Although not without risks, the Rock Harbor Gateway Journey offers paddles entirely along shores protected from open Lake Superior conditions. This trip is suitable for groups new to paddling and for families with children. A string of campgrounds, each within about three miles of the last, accommodates short paddling days and lots of shore time. It offers the thrill of paddling dramatic cliffs and swells along exposed shores, with opportunities to drop back onto protected water if conditions change.

The Rock Harbor Gateway Journey affords a satisfying sampling of Isle Royale's history and culture: the Rock Harbor Lighthouse museum; the traditional Edisen Fishery; an Ojibway Tower hike and climb; and the historic lodge and buildings of Rock Harbor Resort.

Passage to Rock Harbor Marina on either the Copper Harbor or Houghton, Michigan ferries takes three or five hours, respectively. The *Voyager II*'s longer excursion from Grand Portage, Minnesota to Rock Harbor takes seven and a half hours.

A Middle Road Journey: McCargoe Cove to Malone Bay

This moderate-level route expands the Gateway Journey to embrace some of Isle Royale's exposed shores: the Palisades to Blake Point and Middle Island Passage to Saginaw Point, Chippewa Harbor, and Malone Bay. The water distance is 43 miles. Paddlers choosing this route should have rough water experience, solid self-rescue skills, and group practice in assisted rescues. Allow an extra day or two in your schedule for rough seas.

This route features Isle Royale's Five Finger Bay and could encompass visits to historic fishing camps on Crystal Cove, Captain Kidd Island, and

Chippewa Harbor. Paddlers can experience the same vistas that entranced early twentieth-century Belle Isle resort visitors. With favorable wind and seas, this journey could be completed in three to four days. But a tight schedule will require you to by-pass interesting side-trips.

The *Voyager II* ferry, from Grand Portage, Minnesota, will drop your kayaks and gear at the McCargoe Cove Campground dock and pick you up at the Malone Bay dock. If Michigan ferries are more convenient, you'd start your trip in the middle, at Rock Harbor Marina. From there you could paddle out and back to both ends. Or hire water taxi service to drop you in McCargoe Cove and return you from Malone Bay.

Circumnavigation Journey

There is nothing elite in circumnavigating Isle Royale—paddlers accomplish this feat every summer. Still, there is satisfaction in leaving no Isle Royale shore untasted.

The shortest Isle Royale circumnavigation paddling distance is 112 miles. This distance includes a thirteen-mile reach between Huginnin Cove and Little Todd Harbor, where landing options are limited to narrow beaches at the back of deep notches faulted into vertical basalt. Rough seas eliminate even these landing options. Beginning either in Windigo or Rock Harbor, most paddlers circumnavigate Isle Royale clockwise to increase the likelihood that westerly tailwinds will scoot them along this thirteen-mile reach.

There are no campgrounds for thirty-three miles between Malone Bay and Windigo. You'll likely make at least one wild camp behind this shore.

Ferries and Water Taxis

For thousands of years, muscle-powered boats launched from Minnesota's North Shore or the islands along Thunder Bay's outer rim to make the crossing to Isle Royale. Weather was studied. Prayers to the water were sung. Tobacco and agates were offered at the roots of the Little Cedar Tree. These days, we hand our boats and gear to the ferry crew and climb aboard.

Book your tickets as soon as your group has chosen dates and a route. Ferries book months in advance. That said, it is worth checking for last-minute openings. If your planned journey includes a water taxi, also book that well in advance.

The *Ranger III* from Houghton, Michigan

The *Ranger III*, 165 feet long and thirty-four feet wide, is the National Park Service's largest piece of moving equipment. Nine crew members staff the boat, including rangers who can process your permit during transit.

The *Ranger III* leaves the Isle Royale Visitor Center on the Portage Canal in Houghton, Michigan, each Tuesday and Friday morning from late May through early September. Isle Royale drops can be arranged for either Mott Island or Rock Harbor Marina. Return trips are made each Wednesday and Saturday from the Rock Harbor Marina. The parking lot at the dock in Houghton is free for passengers.

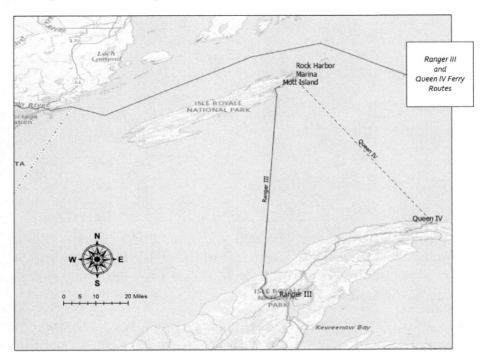

The Isle Royale Queen IV from Copper Harbor, Michigan

The *Isle Royale Queen IV* operates between Copper Harbor, Michigan, and Rock Harbor Marina from mid-May until late September. During the peak season, she leaves each morning except Wednesday to make a four-hour crossing and returns each afternoon. She runs only on Mondays and Fridays during the early and late seasons.

The Grand Portage Isle Royale Transportation Lines

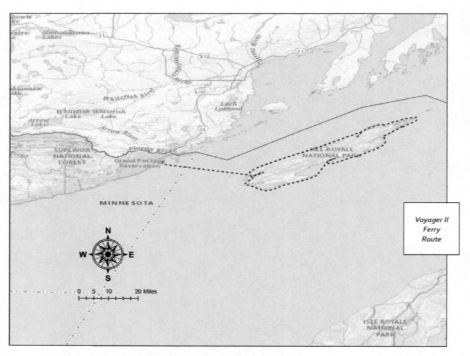

The Sivertson family has operated the Grand Portage Isle Royale Transportation Lines since the *America*'s wreck left Isle Royale commercial fishers without transport for their catch. Sailing dates are from mid-May through late September.

The *Voyager II* leaves from Hat Marina on Minnesota's North Shore on Monday, Wednesday, and Saturday during the peak visitor season, from June to mid-September. More limited service is offered between mid-May and June, and from mid-September to October. After a brief Windigo stop, the *Voyager II* continues along Isle Royale's north shore, making any pre-arranged stops at McCargoe Cove Campground and Belle Isle. It overnights at the Rock Harbor Marina.

On Tuesday, Thursday, and Sunday, the *Voyager II* leaves Rock Harbor to return to Hat Marina, with any pre-planned stops at Daisy Farm, Chippewa Harbor, Malone Bay Campground, or Windigo.

The *Sea Hunter III* sails from early June through early September between Hat Marina and Windigo on Wednesday through Sunday during the peak season and Wednesday, Friday, and Saturday in the early and late season.

Water Taxis

Water taxi service will transport you, your kayaks, and gear from Rock Harbor Marina to Duncan Bay Narrows, Belle Isle, or McCargoe Cove on the north shore, and Moskey Basin, Chippewa Harbor, or Malone Bay along the south shore. A water taxi can also be engaged for a Passage Island trip. Rates depend on the distance.

Book your water taxi well in advance. Service is subject to lake conditions. A taxi won't run when conditions are so rough you don't want to paddle. Make sure the taxi can accommodate your people and boats in a single trip. Cost per person drops significantly when divided among up to six passengers.

Paddling Skills

Scanning an undulating horizon, my body sensed the boat's lift and drop as each swell passed beneath her hull. I was transfixed by waves that surged and kissed the rocks with foamy turmoil. Attention sharpened.

Safely paddling Isle Royale depends on adequate equipment, skills, judgment, and on your ability to anticipate Lake Superior conditions. You'll be moving sixty to a hundred pounds of gear several miles each day. With an efficient stroke, you'll have more fun and be less likely to suffer fatigue or injury. Solid turns, braces, and rescues will give you confidence on crossings, bumpy water, and committed reaches.

Take classes from an experienced coach, join a club, or learn from more experienced friends. Coaches who train coastal kayaking skills will be more helpful than those who coach flat water or white-water skills. Videos, kayaking symposia, and books are other ways to learn. A hired guide is another great option.

Nothing replaces getting on the water. Practice exiting from a capsized boat and scrambling back in with and without assistance. Know the basic T-rescue: how to drain a buddy's kayak quickly and efficiently and then stabilize their boat while they reenter. Practice in swimming pools, warm water, or calm conditions. But to confidently perform a rescue in the kinds of conditions in which a capsize is likely, you must also practice when it is blustery, and the seas are big!

Gear

I'd stayed up late stripping granola bars and macaroni and cheese from their cardboard boxes. I'd Sharpied bags with amounts and cooking times. When morning dawned, we drove to the ferry, unloaded two red plastic boats, and laid them with gear bags and paddles on the dock along the bulky steel hull of the Isle Royale Queen. I parked the car at the edge of a grassed lot, tucked against waist-high daisies.

As I ran back to load and board our ferry I felt the weight of weeks of research, planning, shopping, packing, and a thousand other decisions fall from my mind. I hoped we'd be warm, fed, and happy for our five wilderness days. But regardless, what was laid out on that dock would be everything we had.

Batteries expire. Hatch covers crack. Toggle lines break. Stoves fail. A plastic bottle of soap shatters. Tent poles are forgotten at the last camp. Headlamps are improperly stowed and presumed lost. And somehow, we manage.

A kayak has room for more gear than your backpack. Paddling a hundred pounds—enough for a three-week trip—is doable for most of us. But just because you have space does not mean you should bring more stuff. A heavier boat will be slower. Compressing everything to fit under bulging hatch covers each morning takes time. A lighter boat is faster and more fun. Check out the gear list in the appendix.

You would not start a backpacking trip wearing new boots. Spend time with your gear before you arrive in the wilderness. Know how it works and if it suits you. Test drive your new boat, paddle, dry suit, life jacket, or stove. Set up your new tent in the backyard. Sleep a night in your hammock.

Paddling Gear

An inflated queen mattress under a tumble of sheets pressed against the Belle Isle shelter screen. Fishermen with their motorboats sure know how to be comfortable, I thought. I couldn't have been more wrong.

A day earlier, Camp Host Dave Trigg squinted from the top of Belle Isle's south ridge toward Lane Cove, watching a bulky shape slowly thread Belle Harbor's small islands. The profile matched nothing on Trigg's short mental list of things that would navigate the mile and a half crossing. Not a kayak or canoe. Not a small motorboat. Not even a moose.

As the shape grew closer, the image sharpened. A woman and two children perched atop a pile on the belly of a bulky rectangular raft, moving behind a dark neoprene-encased head. Several minutes later, Trigg met the "boat" as it landed on Belle Isle's pebble beach.

The swimmer peeled a wrist-to-ankle wet suit from his broad shoulders as he described their journey. They had landed at Rock Harbor two days earlier, donned backpacks, and hiked fourteen miles to spend the night at the Lane Cove Campground. The next morning, they tugged a queen-sized mattress from their packs and inflated it with a hand pump. After wrapping their gear carefully to protect the mattress from punctures, both children climbed onto its center. The adults swam the mattress through frigid water for the first half mile. When she grew tired and joined the children, the Coast Guard rescue swimmer pulled them all another mile to their destination.

A US Coast Guard rescue swimmer and former Olympic athlete can make a vessel from a blow-up mattress. The rest of us will have to settle for a boat!

Kayaks

Kayaks come in a range of shapes, sizes, and compositions. My first Isle Royale kayak was sixty-five-pounds of rotomolded plastic. One large cockpit, open from bow to stern, encompassed two seats distributed along a thick steel bar to add rigidity. The boat was beamy enough for a child to dance on its deck. Beamy also meant slow. On recent Isle Royale trips, I've paddled sleeker and lighter British-built composite boats with bulkhead-sealed compartments.

Whatever kayak you choose, it must have either watertight bulkheads or flotation bags. A kayak fifteen to eighteen feet long will track adequately and provide enough room for your gear. Test the seat to be sure it will support several hours of comfortable paddling. Foot pegs are essential for an efficient forward stroke. Adjusted them so your knees are slightly bent, but not locked under the deck. Bow and stern toggles and deck lines make quick, efficient rescues.

Renting a kayak is a great way to determine whether it suits you. Outfitters in Minnesota or Michigan's Upper Peninsula will rent kayaks for multiple days. Expect them to ask you about your kayaking experience, whether you have a solid T-rescue, and to sign a waiver accepting responsibility for any damage to the boat or yourself. Symposia and kayak demo days are other great ways to test boats. Test-drive any boat you consider purchasing in wind and waves.

Skeg or Rudder

With its bow pressed into the water, kayaks turn into the wind like a rooftop weathercock, which lends its name to this tendency. Rudder strokes will compensate for weathercocking, but only at the expense of both speed and your energy, particularly in a boat loaded with gear and supplies. The solution is to pin the kayak's stern with a skeg. A rudder will also do the job, but only by sacrificing fixed foot pegs, which reduces the power of your forward stroke.

Isle Royale water depths change abruptly. When paddling with either a rudder or skeg deployed, be mindful of shallow water. Tug that fin into the boat rather than risk its entrapment between boulders.

Paddles

A paddle you'll enjoy lifting from the water 100 to 300 times an hour is a fine investment. Double-bladed paddles come in varied sizes and shapes, but generally they are either Greenland paddles or Euro blades. The long, skinny Greenland blade provides less resistance and may be more comfortable over a long paddling day. Euro blades offer more power and boat control.

A spare paddle should be attached to your boat deck and easily accessible. Add some reflective tape to the blades to improve visibility. It also helps you sort your paddle from a pile. Marking the paddle shaft to indicate your ideal hand position (shoulder-width apart) is another good idea.

Life Jacket, Spray Skirt, Helmet, Tow Belt

Every Isle Royale paddler must have a Type I life jacket and should wear it whenever they are paddling. Make sure your life jacket works well in your boat and allows your arms to move freely. Tug the straps for a secure fit.

Spray skirts fit snugly around your waist and fasten over the cockpit coaming. In even relatively calm conditions, a wave can dump a few gallons into your cockpit. A spray skirt will also keep you warmer and insects out.

Nylon spray skirts are more comfortable and easier to release. But a neoprene skirt will better resist the pressure to cave under a wave crashing over your deck. It keeps the boat drier. A nylon skirt is adequate for the Gateway Journey; marginal for the Middle Road. Anyone planning the Committed Circumnavigation Journey should paddle with a neoprene skirt.

Unless paddling solo, I bring and wear a tow belt to assist a tired or slow paddler. Although I wear a paddling helmet when surfing or rock gardening, I don't bring one to Isle Royale. In a loaded kayak and an isolated setting, I don't plan to paddle anything I feel I need a helmet for.

Suits Wet and Dry

Open Lake Superior summer water temperatures range from the 40s to the 50s. Spring and fall temperatures are even more bone-achingly chilling and dangerous. Lake Superior water temperatures around Isle Royale also vary widely. Harbors and coves with limited connection to open Lake Superior will be warmer. You might launch onto relatively warm water in Chippewa Harbor, for example, and find yourself on much colder water a few minutes later as you move through its mouth.

Wind pushes warm surface water toward a downwind shore. The upwind shore water will be cold as deeper water rises to replace what was swept away.

The standard advice to dress for the water and use rolls to stay cool on hot days is useful for sport kayaking but make little sense for wilderness touring. Even if you confidently roll a loaded kayak, you don't want to risk your dry equipment to a poorly sealed hatch.

The gold standard for frigid water immersion is a dry suit. These garments seal at the wrist and neck. GORE-TEX dry suits allow sweat to evaporate. Dry suits with attached waterproof socks keep feet dry and warm.

Besides their cost, however, dry suits also have challenges. Latex wrist and neck gaskets are prone to split. While a split gasket can be field-repaired, a repaired gasket is more likely to split again. Furthermore, a taped gasket, worn over days, can produce a painful blister. Dry suits with neoprene rather than latex gaskets won't seal as well but are adequate for an accidental capsize. Neoprene is more durable than latex.

On long crossings or committed reaches, the challenge of peeing in a kayak is different for different bodies. Dry suits can be purchased with either a drop seat, or with a front relief zipper. For those with female anatomy, the front zipper can be used with a female urination device. But an informal survey of woman-identified paddlers tilts toward the drop seat version. On the other hand, I might risk popping my spray skirt on a multi-hour crossing to access a front relief zipper and pee into a bottle. Reaching under my bum to open the longer drop seat zipper in the same situation seems both impractical and insane.

A Farmer John or Farmer Jane wet suit is less expensive than a dry suit. Its neoprene is more durable. Worn over a mid-weight thermal top and under a paddling jacket, it offers a lot of protection in a swim. Feet will get wet. But on a long crossing, if conditions are not too rough, I can pop my spray skirt, unzip the wet suit relief zipper and pee into a bottle without landing. Sometimes that, right there, is my idea of heaven.

I've also paddled Isle Royale wearing fleece layers under waterproof pants and jacket. But such clothing choices should limit our paddling to flat seas and stable weather.

Shoes

You'll want water shoes and another shoe for camps and trails. A sneaker-like shoe designed specifically for water sports has a solid grip and provides better walking, launching, and landing support than neoprene. A reinforced, mostly mesh top allows the shoe to drain and dry quickly. Hiking shoes or boots are nice for trails.

Storm Cag

If you've ever wiggled out of your life jacket without landing to add or remove a layer, you know this is a flat-water endeavor. A garment that can be quickly tugged from a day hatch, slipped over everything, and then secured around the cockpit coaming is magic. On blustery days or in a downpour, pull a storm cag over everything as soon as you land before you get chilled.

Paddling Gloves

The backs of your hands, while paddling, are exposed to intense sun and are prone to burn. Fingerless paddling gloves will protect them. But they also interrupt direct skin-to-paddle blade contact. Blisters may develop where the glove ends on each finger.

Either fingerless or fully fingered neoprene gloves also keep your hands warm. Another warm hand option is pogies—envelopes that Velcro around the paddle shaft. Nestled in their warm, neoprene cocoon, palms will still maintain contact with the paddle shaft. You won't need these, though, except for early or late season trips.

Paddle Floats and Bilge Pumps

A paddle float rescue may be an interesting class exercise, but when you recover in conditions that resulted in a capsize, you need to be ready to dig both paddle blades into the water, not fiddling with a paddle float.

Some folks also find a bilge pump unnecessary. I find it much easier, though, to empty water with a bilge pump than to tip and drain a loaded kayak.

Emergency Signaling Devices

A whistle should be attached to your life jacket to get the attention of someone in your group. A waterproof strobe light, signal horn, and red flares help signal an emergency over longer distances.

Repair Kit

Any multi-day wilderness trip should include a repair kit for your boat, tent, stove, and water filter. A two-liter dry bag will easily contain these items and keep things organized:

- A multipurpose tool with awl and pliers (I keep this in my emergency bag, discussed below)
- Nylon zip ties in an assortment of lengths
- Latex gloves
- 80-grit sandpaper to roughen surfaces before gluing
- Vinyl patches to repair tents, dry bags, and spray skirts
- Aqua seal, which can serve as either an adhesive or a patch for almost anything: a tent fly, hiking boots, or hatch covers
- Tent pole sleeve to slide over a broken pole
- Duct tape wrapped around a Sharpie marker
- Eyeglass screwdriver
- A small cloth for wiping or cleaning
- A spare flexible hatch cover
- A couple of Allen wrenches sized for your boat fittings
- Three or four cotton swabs and toothpicks for cleaning and smearing
- Asphalt tape for boat hull repair
- A small bottle of alcohol for cleaning and drying

- Repair kit (including a spare pump, if appropriate) for fuel stove

- Repair kit for dry suit gaskets

- Spare water pump filter

- Twenty feet of deck line

- Fine net to repair tent screen

A Bail-Out Bag

As a solo kayaker, being stranded without help is something I think about. Even for an evening paddle on my local lake in the middle of Austin, I bring a bail-out bag with a multipurpose tool, a compass, a mylar emergency blanket, matches in a waterproof case, a spoon, salt, and a small bottle of soap. Also inside the bag is a small waterproof box, 1.25 inches by 4.25 inches by 2.5 inches, with Ibuprofen, Imodium, Pepto Bismol tablets, Dramamine, an antihistamine, mole skin, adhesive bandages, tweezers, identification, a twenty-dollar bill, credit card, and foam ear plugs.

Clothing

You'll want cotton for sunning on warm beach afternoons and synthetic or wool layers for chillier days. Bring a fleece or synthetic jacket, rain jacket, and pants. You'll want a brimmed hat that will stay on in the wind to protect your face, and a wool, knit, or fleece hat to keep your head warm.

Shelter

Tents, tarps, bivy sacks, and hammocks each have advantages and disadvantages. A tent is spacious. You can slip into it before mosquitoes emerge and stay snuggled inside until morning.

Sleeping in a bivy sack or hammock offers a special connection to the night. They weigh less and take up less room in your kayak. A hammock provides a comfortable sleeping surface when the alternative is sloped ground or fallen logs. But you will be limited to sites with two properly spaced trees and a clear area between them. A sleeping pad in the hammock is essential for insulation. Bring a hammock screen to keep out mosquitoes. National Park regulations prohibit hanging a hammock in or around a shelter.

A tarp provides shelter for cooking and hanging out on stormy days. If traveling solo, a five-by-seven-foot tarp is plenty. For a group, a larger tarp is nice.

A small, foldable camp chair weighs less than two pounds and tucks neatly into the space beside a skeg box.

Sleeping Bags

A sleeping bag designed for backpacking rather than camping will weigh less and pack smaller. Choose one with synthetic fill that, unlike down, will keep you warm even when wet. Average Isle Royale low temperatures from June through September are forty-eight to fifty-two degrees, so a summer-weight bag is adequate. Pack your sleeping bag in a waterproof compression sack.

Sleeping Pads

Closed-cell foam sleeping pads take up more room in your boat than you can spare. Air or self-inflating pads are comfortable, lightweight, and compact. Some contain insulation or reflective material to increase warmth. Bring a repair kit.

Charts, Maps, Compasses, and Electronics

Accurate charts, detailed maps, and a slew of electronic devices are available to support your Isle Royale navigation. The National Oceanic and Atmospheric Agency (NOAA) publishes Isle Royale Chart No. 14976. Third-party vendors will print the chart onto waterproof paper and ship it to you. Allow a couple of weeks for delivery.

I also recommend the National Geographic Trails Illustrated Map for Isle Royale National Park. It provides detailed topographic, campground, and trail information, including distances. It names islands and topographic features not named on the NOAA chart. It also lists water route distances between major island points.

Compass

A compass mounted on the deck of your kayak provides information regarding the direction your boat is pointing without taking your hands from your paddle. If your boat is not equipped with a deck-mounted compass, you can purchase one that straps on. A hand-held compass is also useful to take bearings without turning your boat and while hiking. I keep one in my life jacket pocket.

Electronics

Escaping an electronically connected world is one of Isle Royale's features. But you are probably going to bring some electronic devices. Here are things to consider.

For many years, on a rare day, with stars aligned and perhaps muttering the proper spell, you could bounce a cell phone call from Isle Royale off a Canadian tower. But you were just as likely to get crickets. Even without cell phone service, however, a smartphone can take photographs, shoot video, and store maps, plant guides, and first aid instructions. As mainland cell service has improved, you might send or receive text messages from locations along Isle Royale's southern, northern, or western shores.

A GPS (Global Positioning System) device or a satellite communicator locates its position based on receiving satellite signals. If a map is pre-loaded, it can display your location. Your smartphone does this, too.

A personal locater beacon will send an emergency message with your position to local law enforcement, search and rescue, or the Coast Guard. Their function is limited and straightforward, and they do not require a paid subscription. You get no message in return, and you can't send a custom message. If you carry these devices, do not let them lull you into paddling conditions beyond your skill level. Take full responsibility for your own safety.

One-way satellite communicators allow you to send messages and two-way satellite communicators allow you to send and receive messages. They can send your location at specified intervals to a map where friends and family can follow your course. These devices require a subscription data service similar to your cell phone service.

VHF Marine Radio

A floating, waterproof, handheld VHF radio offers weather forecasts and the ability to communicate with boats and park rangers within line-of-sight. Isle Royale's ridges, however, will block VHF communication and weather forecast reception. Reception is improved from a high point or out on the water. As a recreational boater traveling within the United States, you may use a marine VHF radio without a license. Park rangers and larger boats will monitor VHF Channel 16. Certain VHF channels are designated for critical safety and information purposes. Do not interfere with or interrupt these official communications.

Solar Panel

A small solar panel can charge a battery pack, cell phone, camera, or electronic book reader through a USB outlet. With an automotive auxiliary power socket, it can also recharge your VHF radio. This VHF radio recharging capability is important on long trips to maintain access to weather reports.

Water Filtration

Potable water is only available on Isle Royale at Rock Harbor and Windigo. Elsewhere your water supply is Lake Superior. You will need either a pump or gravity water filter to disinfect drinking water. A sterilizing pen is inadequate for tapeworm and giardia cysts. Bring a spare filter cartridge.

Stoves

On lichen-covered rocks above Malone Bay, I pressed my gasoline stove's fuel pump plunger and felt no resistance. What?!? The pump was broken, and I was utterly baffled about how to repair it. Our group had another propane stove. I wouldn't go hungry. But what if I had been paddling solo?

Returning home, I purchased a spare stove fuel pump for my stove and now keep it in my repair bag.

The stove fuel debate is hot. Propane is easy to use and quiet. But it is difficult to gauge how much fuel remains in a partially used container. White gas fuel is easier to budget. You can bring exactly the amount you need. Weighing fuel, container, and stove together, white gas is also lighter.

If propane is your choice, make sure you bring canisters that match your stove. I've met more than one camper wandering a campground hoping to find someone with an extra canister that matches their stove because the one they brought didn't.

Pots, Pans, and Other Kitchen Items

Pots and pans designed for backpacking have collapsible handles. They'll fit more easily into your hatch. Stainless steel doesn't leach aluminum and is less expensive than titanium. The number and size of pots you need will depend on your group size and menu complexity. Paddling solo, I bring one quart pot and a small nonstick skillet. For two or three people, bring another half-gallon pot. For four to six paddlers, bring another one-gallon pot.

Besides pots and pans, you'll want one large spoon for stirring and a plastic spatula if you intend to make pancakes, skillet brownies, or scones. A small, backpacking cutting board might be handy and a serving ladle with a folding handle keeps things tidy. Bring a small thermos for a hot beverage on a cold, damp shore break. For cleanup, a small plastic pot scraper works better than sponges that stay wet and greasy.

Lights

On a midsummer day, sunrise to sunset spans sixteen hours and twilight lasts from dusk to dawn. You may never experience darkness. Supplemental light is handy, however, as the year wanes into September.

Even in summer, inside shelters can be dark. A headlamp leaves your hands free. Drop it into a Nalgene bottle for a soft dinner table glow. A red-light option preserves night vision and is less disturbing to wildlife.

First Aid

Situations on Isle Royale requiring evacuation are rare. A well-stocked first aid kit handles most bumps and scrapes. Keep your first aid kit in a dry bag and mark it clearly. If you are hurt, you don't want to be the only person who can locate supplies.

Your kit might include:

- Antiseptic wipes
- Antibacterial ointment
- Assorted adhesive bandages
- Butterfly bandages/ adhesive wound-closure strips
- Gauze pads
- Nonstick sterile pads
- Medical adhesive tape
- Moleskin and a blister kit
- Ibuprofen or other pain relief medication
- Insect bite treatment
- Red clay to extract toxins
- Poison ivy/ poison oak wash and treatment
- Broad-spectrum antibiotic pills and creams
- Antidiarrheals
- Triangular bandage with safety pins
- An antihistamine for allergic reactions

- Fine-point tweezers to remove splinters

- A first aid manual or information cards

- Elastic wrap

- Throat lozenges

- Paramedic shears

- Cotton-tipped swabs

- Oral thermometer

- Irrigation syringe

- Nitrile medical gloves

- CPR mask

- Pencil and paper for notes

- Temporary filling material

- Injectable epinephrine for severe allergic reactions

Food

Some paddlers happily devour the same menu every day. Others relish an exquisite five-course meal in the wild.

If your paddling team is larger than one, decide whether meals will be communal or individual. One compromise is individual breakfasts and lunches, and communal dinners. If you are bringing meals for others, ask how much they eat. Some of my paddling buddies eat twice as much as me.

You can provision your trip from shelf-stable food available in many grocery stores. Boxed macaroni and cheese dinners, Indian food in foil packages, ramen, instant rice, dried falafel, dried hummus, dried tomatoes, basil pesto, tuna, salmon, and chicken in sealed foiled packets, granola, oatmeal, dried fruits, and nuts provide everything you need for simple and satisfying meals. Coffee and dry milk also come in instant varieties. It is worth shopping your local food cooperative or organic grocery store for higher quality and a larger variety of these staples. Canned food is heavy and difficult to store. Save them for your car camping trip.

Over Lake Superior's chilling water, temperatures in your boat hull stay cool enough, even on warm summer days, for cabbage, radicchio, onion, peppers, and carrots. Whole carrots last longer than processed "baby" carrots. Cheese, summer sausage, and mustard will last at least three weeks, if kept out of the sun on shore breaks. Toss canned beverages into a net and chill them in the lake.

Another menu option is freeze-dried meals. These meals are better for breakfast and dinner since you won't typically unpack a stove for lunch. One appeal is ease: pour boiling water into a foil bag, stir, and wait. Spoon them from the bag and eliminate cleanup.

If you are a foodie with time ahead to prepare, dehydrated ingredients can improve your meal experience. Dehydrated stews with vegetables or small meat chunks take ten to fifteen minutes to rehydrate. Putting the dehydrated food in a Nalgene bottle at lunch and allowing it to soak over the afternoon will shorten the cooking time.

Packaged your food carefully to keep it dry and organized. Transfer boxed food into a zip-top bag. Write cooking instructions on the bag using a permanent marker or snip instructions from the box and tuck them into the bag. Pack cheese (which will inevitably separate in the heat), summer sausage, and cookies in a zip-top bag. A small, soft-sided lunch box can store each day's lunch beside small bottles of olive oil and mustard. It will help keep dark chocolate from melting into a gooey puddle.

Vegetarians

Kayaking Coach Alec Bloyd-Peshkin provisions vegetarian menus from a mix of grocery store items and dehydrated recipes he prepares in advance, aiming for ten to fifteen minutes of cooking time for dinner, which provides some flexibility without being too extravagant with fuel.

He recommends these vegetarian wilderness options:

- Boxed macaroni and cheese supplemented with extra cheese and dehydrated vegetables: onion, carrot, broccoli, bell pepper, yellow squash, zucchini, tomatoes, and garlic.

- Aseptically packaged tofu.

- Dehydrated oyster mushrooms.

- Dehydrated sauerkraut finely chopped to garnish a salad.

- Stew made of white beans, tomatoes, greens, onions, and garlic. Cook, dehydrate, and store the beans separately from the rest of the ingredients.

Fishing and Foraging

Our quarter-mile ramble from Edisen Fishery to the Rock Harbor Lighthouse became even slower as we moved from the shaded forest into a sunny thimbleberry field. I turned to see my three-year-old daughter painted, chin to waist, in their purple juice.

Isle Royale's most significant food offering is fish. Both Lake Superior and the inland lakes provide a bountiful, fresh meal for those initiated in fishing ways. It is legal to fish the interior lakes without a license. Bring a Michigan fishing license if you plan to fish in Lake Superior.

Next to fish, the most commonly harvested Isle Royale food is thimbleberries, abundant along the woodland trails. They are delicious by the handful or tossed into a cup of granola. Cook them into pancakes or simmer them lightly with butter and maple syrup and drizzle over chocolate brownies.

Raspberries are common in open areas and behind several beaches. Blueberries stud ridges. Strawberries pack a sweet, tangy punch. Look for them on vines across rock outcrops. Harvest dandelion greens from along trails and sauté them for a bit of something fresh with dinner. Scrape beach peas from their shells and enjoy their raw, crisp sweetness.

Everything Will Get Wet

You've packed your gear into dry bags and squished out the air. You've carefully folded their tops the prescribed three times and sealed them. You've double-checked hatch cover seals. It is a sunny day, and you don't plan to go far.

But the roll of entropy's dice means everything eventually gets wet. Black mold finds life on wrinkled book pages. Journal ink smears. Binocular lenses fog. Charts emerge from a dry suit pocket in tatters. If it exists, purchase the waterproof version of everything. Seal critical items in a couple of layers of waterproof protection. Buy charts on waterproof material or paint the paper with a map-sealing fluid and lay them into a waterproof chart case. Don't take what you can't afford to lose.

Large, rubbery dry bags used in canoes won't fit efficiently into kayak hatches. You'll want smaller, more flexible ones. Compressible waterproof stuff sacks are useful for sleeping bags and clothing.

Information, Lodging, Food, and Supplies

Visitor Centers

Unless you arrived on the *Ranger III,* your first stop will be the National Park Visitor Center at either Rock Harbor or Windigo. There you will pay your Isle Royale daily park use fee, $7 per person, as of 2021. There is no fee for children fifteen or younger. If your trip will be longer than eight days, a $60 Isle Royale season pass, valid from April 16 through October 31, is cheaper than the daily fees. Purchase a season pass in advance or from either of the visitor centers. Starting in the summer of 2022, however, the park will be cashless. Annual, military, and senior passes cover fees for the pass holder and up to three additional visitors in their party. Both visitor centers stock Isle Royale-themed books, posters, maps, and charts.

Campgrounds

To minimize human impact, Isle Royale National Park requires campers who can access campgrounds to use them. Every campground has at least one pit toilet (but not always toilet paper), tent pads, and picnic tables. Many of the lakeshore campgrounds also have Adirondack shelters. With a roof,

Huginnin Cove Camp

floor, three walls of wood, and one of screen, a shelter makes setting up camp easy. They also protect against mosquitoes or weather.

None of the campgrounds have electricity, and only Rock Harbor and Windigo provide potable water. If all shelters and tent sites are occupied, negotiate a share or paddle to another campground.

Rock Harbor

Rock Harbor's hotel-style rooms accommodate up to four in two double beds, with a private bath. There are also twenty cottages, with private baths, kitchenettes, utensils, and dishes to accommodate six. A dining hall and the adjacent Greenstone Grill serve meals. The dockside store sells camping, hiking, boating supplies, limited groceries, freeze-dried foods, beer, wine, fishing licenses, and shower tokens. There is a coin-operated washer and dryer.

Windigo

Windigo's two rustic camper cabins accommodate six with two bunk beds, a futon sofa, tables, chairs, electrical outlets, and lights. Each cabin has a picnic table, propane grill, a nearby spigot, and an outdoor toilet. A limited selection of groceries, sandwiches, beer, wine, camping supplies, stove fuel, fishing licenses, and gifts can be purchased at the Windigo Store.

Go

Rocking your wilderness experience means being comfortable in a range of weather and sea conditions. It means venturing out of your comfort zone and safely into your adventure zone. It includes staying healthy, nourished, rested, and hydrated. It also includes healthy group dynamics and deepening relationships with your paddling team and yourself.

Beginning

From Brockway Mountain, sixty miles of Lake Superior's shore stretched to the western horizon. After three days of the relentless thrum of highway travel, my ears rang in the stillness. My feet barely connected with the earth.

The breeze was fresh. Gold and crimson flashed in trees arching the narrow road from Houghton to Copper Harbor, at the tip of the Keweenaw Peninsula. The Isle Royale Queen's steel hull snuggled against her dock in the fading twilight.

My mind roiled with questions, and my stomach responded with churning anxiousness. Had I arrived too late in the season? Would the weather be unstable? Temperatures too cool for my thin Texas blood? What if I spilled fuel and had no way to cook? Or spilled my only bottle of fountain pen ink? I could just turn around and drive back to Texas. No one but me was invested in this trip.

Crossing

Arrive at the ferry dock early. Lift your boats from the dock into the crew's waiting hands on the ferry's top deck. Pass your neatly packed gear bags and the tumble of paddles and fuel bottles. Then climb aboard for the crossing.

Even on sunny days, Lake Superior's chilly water and your ferry speed will make the crossing chilly. Layer up with fleece, a warm hat, and a rain jacket or plan to be confined in the boat's cabin. Bring your water bottle and some snacks.

Arriving

Crossing from Minnesota's North Shore, your first glimpse of Isle Royale's archipelago will be the Rock of Ages Lighthouse. It rises from an iron base barely bigger than its basalt foundation. Its stark white walls, punctuated by black windows, rise eighty-seven feet.

At the head of Washington Harbor, you'll disembark at the Windigo ranger station. If you cross from Houghton or Copper Harbor, Michigan, you will arrive at the Rock Harbor Visitor Center.

At either landing, park staff will gather everyone on the dock to review leave no trace principles and check your party's drinking water filter. Inside the visitor center, they will note your intended camping locations on a permit and tuck it into a zip-top bag with a long twist tie. You'll wire your permit to your boat and your tent or shelter door handle each night. If your journey includes camping outside designated campgrounds, you will read and sign an additional backcountry permit.

The park will use your permit to monitor campground use, deliver emergency messages, and find lost campers. But you are not obligated to follow its itinerary.

Respect Isle Royale

We are accountable to all beings for minimizing our impact, for preserving and passing forward what we love.

Bring everything with as little waste as possible. Leave boxes and extra packaging at home. Bring a lined dry bag to carry your trash off the Island. Trash includes cans and bottles, but also the micro-bits: twist ties, bottle caps, and snack bar wrappers. Carry out all toilet paper except what you drop into pit toilets.

Use pit toilets where they are available. Put nothing into them other than bodily waste and toilet paper. If there is no pit toilet, do not leave or bury toilet paper. Tuck it into a designated zip-top bag.

Handwashing is pro-social behavior. Set up a handwashing station at least seventy-five steps from Lake Superior, inland lakes, streams, marshes, and campsites. Use a strainer or scraper to remove food bits and pack them out. Use soap sparingly. Pour any soapy water on soil rich with organic material, not onto gravel or stone. Hot water is hard on plants and soil microbes. Let it cool a bit before pouring it out.

Travel and camp on durable surfaces. Use maintained trails and campsites. Step where lichen and plants are already worn from the rock. Be gentle.

Pick berries. Pick friends. Leave flowers, stones, and all relics.

Campfires deplete deadwood that would otherwise replenish soil nutrients. Fire damages rock for millennia. The National Park allows cooking only on stoves. Build fires only where a metal ring or grill has been provided. Use dry wood no thicker than your wrist.

Do not disturb or feed any wildlife. Loons may abandon shoreline nests when approached too closely. During the loon nesting season, from May 1 through July 15, stay at least 150 feet from small islands. If a loon cries, you are too close.

There are no bears on Isle Royale, but turn your back for a moment, and a jay, deer mouse, or chipmunk will scramble across your picnic table, scouting for a bit of cheese, granola, chocolate, or trail mix. Avoid spilling and don't store food inside a tent. Secure it in a shelter, in a sealed kayak hatch, or suspend it from a high branch.

Bull thistle and zebra mussels have invaded Isle Royale. Minimize their spread by cleaning your boots, gear, and boats of plants, seeds, fish, animals, dirt, and mud before your arrival on the Island. Clean boats and fishing gear if you move between Lake Superior and inland lakes.

Operating drones on park land or waters is prohibited.

Weather

An eighteen-knot northeaster drove waves and tumbled gravel. There was no reason to get up. Snuggled in my sleeping bag in Belle Isle Shelter #6, I glanced toward the beach as a head and red life jacket glided above the alders. Moments later, a second paddler scooted onto shore. Adrenalized, giddy laughter rippled across the grassy meadow. I rose to greet the new arrivals.

A seventeen-foot aluminum canoe had been pulled up and tipped against the alders. Wow! These were rough conditions for an open boat. Both Joe and Jerry were experienced Isle Royale paddlers. But their camp in Lane Cove, had offered no hint of open lake conditions. So they had broken camp early and launched. A couple of waves had washed over Jerry's gunwales. He celebrated his safe landing with a pull of cognac from a plastic Coke bottle.

Nothing is more significant to a kayaker's experience of Isle Royale than weather. Winds blow predominantly from the southwest but can come from any direction. Northeast or east winds swirl colder arctic air. Spring and fall storms or a summer squall regularly spin winds up to thirty knots. Eighty knot winds and twenty-foot seas have wrecked Lake Superior's largest boats.

On a typical summer morning, winds pick up about 10 am and peak in midafternoon. As the sun sinks behind treetops, winds and waves settle. The Lake is often alluringly quiet just as dinner steams from the cooking pot.

Despite these general patterns, however, Isle Royale weather is full of surprises. Winds and storm-driven waves can arise day or night. Check marine weather forecasts each morning and evening, and before making a committed or open water crossing.

Besides wind speed, duration, and fetch, waves are shaped by the surrounding land topography and lake floor. The narrowing of a cove or a shallowing lake bottom compresses each wave's energy. Waves respond by becoming steeper until they break, releasing a turbulent cascade of energy.

Points can also create turbulence, as wave energies from two directions collide. After paddling smooth conditions in a ridge lee, you can round a point into the full brunt of chest-high waves. Conditions offshore may also be radically different from those near shore. Slip beyond a protected lee and wind will propel you toward the open lake.

Navigation

Fog cloaked West Caribou Island. Rock Harbor was weirdly silent as Lee and I spread our chart across the shelter floor. We measured three bearings. From West Caribou Island's northwest tip, 220 degrees across Middle Passage would bring us to the lighthouse beach. There, we would turn left toward the tip of its rocky point. From the point, a bearing of 170 degrees for thirty minutes should bring Miner's Point into view. On a bearing of 185 degrees from Miner's Point, the Saginaw Point day marker should be visible in another twenty minutes.

We packed our boats, slipped off the sand beach behind the dock, and floated into the embrace of a gray world. Dark spruce tops were barely discernible above my right shoulder as we skirted the ridge marking one shore of the cut into Conglomerate Bay. Treetops faded as we crossed the bay's mouth, abandoning us to the mystery of nothingness.

Where are you? How far can you travel before lunch? What sea conditions might you expect as you round the next point? Should you turn back? Seafaring folk have asked these questions for thousands of years. They've sought answers in stars, in wind and waves, in clouds and compasses, in sextants and hour glasses. One of my kayaking coaches navigates by "keeping land off my shoulder."

Navigating Isle Royale is relatively easy. Points, islands, rocky outcrops, and shoals make distinctive markers. There are no tides or tidal currents to consider. It is a great place to deepen your navigation skills.

You can download maps into an InReach device and satellites will orient your every moment. It's not a bad option. For extended trips, a small solar panel will recharge its batteries. But there is something profoundly satisfying about chart and compass navigation. The scope of a day's journey is more tangible from a chart laid across polished pebbles. Without digital distractions, I know better where I am.

If you choose to navigate with the basic tools of chart, compass, and a timepiece, all three should be accessible from your kayak seat with a glance. Slip a chart beneath deck bungies. Strap a watch on your wrist or life jacket shoulder strap. Mount or strap a compass to your deck. Slip a hand compass into a life jacket pocket to quickly take a bearing.

The Isle Royale NOAA Marine Chart No. 14976 focuses on shores, rocks, and bathymetry. It displays navigation markers--buoys, lighthouses, radio towers--and near shore topography. It also marks shore campgrounds and trails.

Keep a record of launch and landing times. Use time and distance traveled to calculate speed. Estimate distance traveled and your location based on paddling time and your assumed speed. This practice is useful along Isle Royale's relatively featureless north or southwest shores. Compare your estimated and actual locations. Are they close?

Packing

A well-packed boat, with everything you need to survive and be comfortable, is a feeling of freedom and independence. You did test pack, right? You pulled everything into the garage, dining room, or front yard and loaded it into your boat? A test pack is where you find out whether you have room for the flower guide, the geology book, *and* a novel.

Space for gear storage is available in the front hatch, rear hatch, and day hatch, between your seat and the day hatch bulkhead and between your foot pegs and the front hatch bulkhead. If your boat has no bulkheads, you'll stash gear in waterproof bags into your kayak's bow and stern. In the event of a capsize, however, items stored in the cockpit may fall out. Ensure no gear bag straps or fasteners could entrap you in a wet exit.

Reserve your fore deck for a spare paddle, map, compass, and possibly a water bottle or bailing pump. Keep your rear deck clear for a scramble or assisted rescue.

Distribute weight to balance your boat bow to stern and port to starboard. Optimize your stability and turns by stowing heavy items like water and fuel near the hull and close to the cockpit. You'll need to use narrow spaces at the bow and between the skeg box and hull for skinny items. Fasten them to a length of paracord and fish them out with a tug.

If you plan precisely where in your kayak each item goes, you can haul gear from your camp and lay it next to that part of your boat. Your sunblock won't end up in the bow, requiring you to unpack your sleeping bag, sleeping pad, and tent to slather it on after lunch.

After a couple of days, you'll have your packing system dialed in. The ritual of loading your boat the same way each morning helps you realize your water filter is still dangling from a birch branch.

Launching and Landing

Isle Royale offers few sand beaches. You will often land on rock or gravel. Islands or the rocky ridges of its northeastern end shelter protected landings from Lake Superior waves. Southwestern and northwestern shores are more exposed.

Unload your boat on the beach each evening and carry it above any level where wind-driven waves might float it. Tie it. In the morning, lift the unloaded boat and bring it to the water's edge. If you lay your kayak parallel to the water or prop the water end on a log, gear won't slide along the tilted hull while you load.

Portage

After a mirror-smooth crossing from Copper Harbor, the Isle Royale Queen dropped us with our two boats and gear on the Rock Harbor dock. It was me who'd studied Jim DuFresne's guide and made our plan.

We would carry boats and gear across the quarter-mile asphalt sidewalk, paddle to the other shore of Tobin Harbor, and make the Duncan Portage. The Duncan Bay end of the portage would offer sheltered access to Isle Royale's iconic Five Finger Bay. Jim Dufresne described the Duncan Portage as the most difficult on the Island. But only 0.8 miles long, how hard could it be?

"Let's portage the boats loaded," was evidence of my disconnection from reality. Dave gave me an eye roll. But he helped cram everything into the two plastic hulls. Even the two-year-old sensed we were venturing into uncharted territory. Geneva insisted on riding into whatever our future held glued to my hip.

When the boats were finally loaded with all our gear, I wrapped one arm around her waist, bent and tugged a stern toggle. A hundred-twenty pounds of boat and gear did not budge. Twenty minutes later, and everything unpacked, David and I each lifted an end of an empty boat and began the quarter-mile walk. It took five trips before both boats and all our gear lined the Tobin Harbor shore. I should have known then.

We reloaded the boats and slipped them onto the water. Wooded shores clamored with birdsong. Squirrel chatter framed the open lake. We were living my dream.

Five minutes later, we landed on Tobin Harbor's north shore at the wooden post marking the portage. We unloaded the boats again. With Dave at the bow, me at the stern, and Geneva again fixed to my hip, we lifted sixty-five pounds of empty plastic to our shoulders. When we'd carried it as far as I could up the ridge, we laid it on the bunchberries that edged trail and walked back for the next boat. Back and forth again for several more loads of gear.

When everything was together, we repeated the process, lifting the heaviest boat to our shoulders and walking the trail as far as I could carry it. Then the lighter boat and another several trips for gear. We crawled toward the top of each ridge, certain this would be the one to offer a view of Isle Royale's north shore and Lake Superior stretching to the Canadian coast. But as afternoon light waned, while each ridge summit presented only a view of the next, I finally accepted that the Duncan Portage was beyond us. We turned back.

Unlike Minnesota's Boundary Waters culture, portaging is not a kayaking tradition. Rather than a single bulky portage pack, kayaking's skinny gear packages are sized to nestle into the vessel's narrow, rounded hull. Despite these challenges, and our failed Duncan Bay attempt, most of the Island's portages could be accomplished with kayaks, provided your party includes at least someone to carry the bow and someone else under the stern. Several short Isle Royale portages access quiet, isolated bays when paddling around a point would expose you to rough conditions.

Three Journeys

The three journeys described below are suitable for paddlers with different skills and experience levels. The Gateway Rock Harbor Journey is advisable for beginning paddlers, groups with children, and those with tight schedules. Paddlers undertaking the Middle McCargoe Cove to Malone Bay journey should be comfortable in two-foot waves and making headway in winds up to fifteen knots. They should have the endurance to paddle fifteen miles in a day; and solid self- and assisted T-rescues. Paddlers undertaking a Committed Circumnavigation Journey should be able to make headway in winds up to twenty knots and have the endurance to paddle twenty miles in a day.

These trip recommendations assume favorable conditions during summer months. Spring and fall storms or sudden summer squalls can turn a beginner's trip into one suitable only for advanced paddlers. Schedule a couple extra days to sit out unfavorable weather.

The Gateway Rock Harbor Journey

After two days of rain and waves, the third morning dawned clear and calm. We carried boats to the beach, loaded gear, and launched. After a short paddle, the Three Mile Campground shelters welcomed us from the top of smooth, glacier-buffed basalt.

We landed and made camp. Then, for a while, we laid on the rock, lizards soaking in sun.

But soon, through the gap between Mott and Hill Islands, Lake Superior summoned us. We traced wave-scrubbed rocks along Mott's southeast shore; peered through narrow fault slots to beaches of round cobble. A dizzying pattern of reefs and faulted stone slipped sixty feet under our hulls. Lunch, on a cobble beach, was sliced summer sausage on slightly squashed whole wheat bread, mustard, and cheese gone soft and oily. Granola bars were dessert.

Arnold Johnson's Belle on the Edisen Fishery Shore

Rock Harbor offers a distilled essence of the best of Isle Royale. Relics of Isle Royale's cultural history dot Rock Harbor's shores. The Scoville Point Trail skirts Anishinaabe copper pits. Daisy Farm occupies an 1800s mining camp site. The Rock Harbor Lighthouse is a museum of shipwreck history. Edisen fishery represents the Island's commercial fishing culture.

Sift for greenstones on the sunny lighthouse beach. Wander through the twenty-five-year-old moose antler garden behind the Bangsund cabin. Poke your head through the doorway of a fishing cabin. Turn the crank on a fisher's grinding stone. You might study black flecks, insects caught by carnivorous plants along Raspberry Island's swamp walks, or rock garden Mott Island's outer shore.

This trip is suitable for anyone with the capacity and desire to paddle a kayak. Islands protect the harbor from the brunt of Lake Superior conditions. Distances between camps are short, leaving time to hike, explore, or read.

Portage Lake and the Scoville Point lava flows form Rock Harbor's north shore. Its south shore, from Middle Island Passage's rock spires to the far-flung tip of South Government Island, is emergent sections of Portage Lake flows. Steep edges of these primordial flows are evident in cliffs along West Caribou Island's northwest shore and between Edisen Fishery and the Rock Harbor Lighthouse beach. Mott Island's outer shore is formed from their sloped flow surface.

The spine of Mott and East and West Caribou Islands is volcanic conglomerate rock. Snug Harbor, Three Mile Campground, Daisy Farm and Moskey Basin beaches are cut into Isle Royale's softer sedimentary rock.

Paddling the outer shores of islands that form Rock Harbor's south edge offers the opportunity to experience a landscape shaped by the full force of open Lake Superior water. Winter storms pound these cliffs, strip low-lying vegetation, and expose a maze of rocks, slots, and pools. Mott, the longest island, is only a mile and a half. If Lake Superior's sea conditions change, you can quickly drop back onto Rock Harbor's protected water.

While this introductory journey is suitable for beginning paddlers and families, it is not without risks. Even in the harbor, water can be dangerously cold in a capsize. Predominant southwest winds align along its nine-mile fetch to generate waves and a progress-slowing headwind.

Paddles

I slipped onto a pool less than an hour's paddle from Rock Harbor's busy marina. Only rain had touched the reindeer lichen on its rocky shore. Purple harebells nodded against a breeze. Over the rumble of waves on the lakeside rock, above the gentle lap of ripples under the boat, was the quiet clickity-clickity of flying grasshoppers.

Scoville Point

The Scoville Point paddle is suitable for beginners on calm days with forecasted stable weather. Any wind or swell on Lake Superior, however, might produce challenging conditions as you round the point.

From the Snug Harbor beach in front of the Greenstone Grill, paddle around the SS *America* dock at the end of the peninsula to your left and follow the shore northeast. Hotel room balconies rim the first hundred yards, and then the shore becomes wild. The next two miles are a montage of rocky beaches and polished cliffs. You might see occasional hikers on the Scoville Point Trail, but you are unlikely to see other paddlers.

Nearing Scoville Point, Lake Superior's swell swirls around rock etched by winter's power. Waves undulate beneath your boat. A few more strokes pull you onto Tobin Harbor's quiet water.

Tobin Harbor

Smith and Newman Islands guard Tobin Harbor's entrance, guaranteeing millpond conditions. The harbor is five miles long and less than a quarter mile wide. Your attention is free to engage with its rocky shore, stony bottom, and shimmering greens of western cedar, spruce, aspen, and birch that edge the shore.

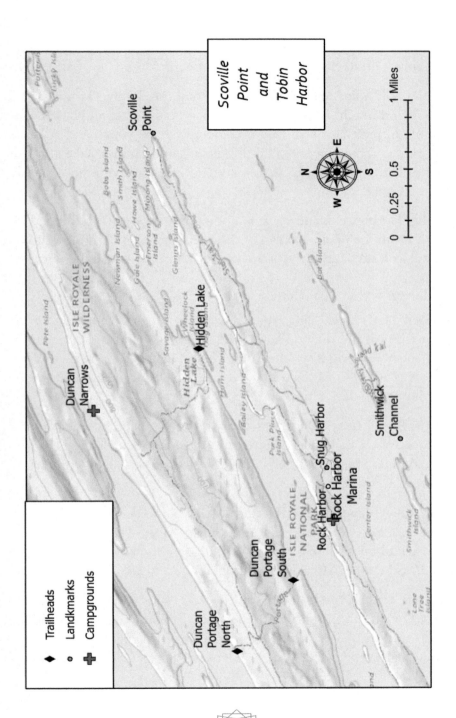

Scoville
Point
and
Tobin
Harbor

Trailheads
Landmarks
Campgrounds

Scoville
Point

Duncan
Narrows

ISLE ROYALE
WILDERNESS

Hidden Lake

Pete Island

Newman Island
Bobs Island
Smith Island
Howe Island
Gate Island
Emerson Island
Mooning Island
Glenys Island

Savage Island

Wheelock Island

Hidden
Lake

Tooth Island

Bailey Island

Park Place
Island

Duncan
Portage
South

ISLE ROYALE
NATIONAL
PARK

Duncan
Portage
North

Portage

Rock Harbor
Rock Harbor
Marina

Snug Harbor

Smithwick
Channel

Dot Island

Raspberry Island

Bird Island

Center Island

Smithwick
Island

Lone
Tree
Island

N W E S

0   0.25   0.5   1 Miles

Before the National Park was established, this sheltered harbor was a popular location for private summer cottages. Now all but a handful of their simple cabins and docks have faded back into the forest.

One and a half miles west from Scoville Point, on Tobin Harbor's north shore, is a sand beach. Land, tug your kayak onto the grass and head up the trail. In June, pink lady's slipper orchids may edge your path. A mama moose with her nursing calf may be grazing on Hidden lake's aquatic vegetation The 1.0-mile hike to Lookout Louise ends with an expansive view of the Canadian shore.

The Tobin Harbor seaplane dock is another mile beyond the Hidden Lake trailhead. From the dock, you can portage your boat a quarter mile along a paved trail to Rock Harbor. Or retrace your paddle and skip the portage.

Rock Harbor Marina to Daisy Farm

Most Rock Harbor paddling routes begin on Snug Harbor's fine gravel beach in front of the dining hall. In the 1990s, sail and motor yachts sat cheek-to-jowl with modest open motorboats in adjacent berths. While luxury yachts are now less common, you might still paddle behind one and imagine life on its elegant deck.

The north Rock Harbor shore is dense forest punctuated by smooth basalt outcrop. Across a half mile of open water, Smithwick, Shaw, Davidson, Outer and Inner Hill, Mott, East and West Caribou Islands protect the harbor from Lake Superior's raucous seas.

Of these outer islands, only Mott and Davidson are occupied. Mott is the National Park Service's working island. Single-story government office and warehouse buildings circle a grass lawn leading to the large dock where the *Ranger III* is berthed. Working barges tuck into a nearby harbor.

One of two Three Mile Campground docks nestles into a sandy cove on Rock Harbor's north shore, about three miles from the marina. A cove-side trail lined with raspberry brambles leads to several shelters hidden in the woods. A quarter-mile west, a second dock protrudes from a basalt nose.

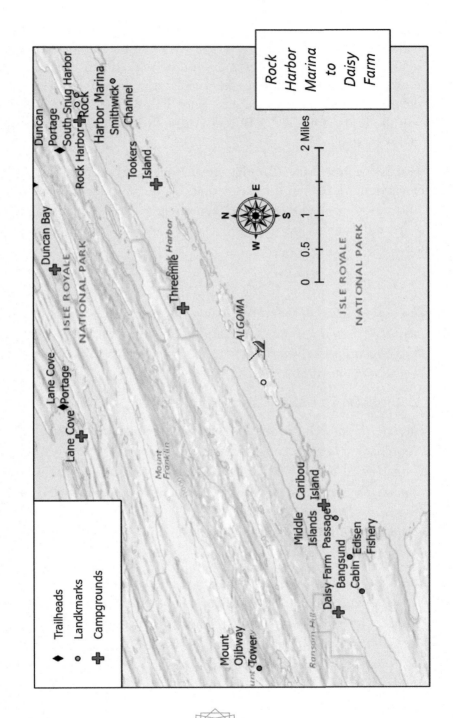

Rock
Harbor
Marina
to
Daisy
Farm

Trailheads
Landmarks
Campgrounds

Duncan
Portage
South Snug Harbor
Rock Harbor ROCK
Harbor Marina
Smithwick
Tookers
Island
Channel

Duncan Bay

ISLE ROYALE
NATIONAL PARK

Threemile Harbor

ALGOMA

Lane Cove
Portage
Lane Cove

Mount
Franklin

N
W   E
S

0   0.5   1   2 Miles

ISLE ROYALE
NATIONAL PARK

Middle   Caribou
Islands   Island

Daisy Farm Passage
Bangsund
Cabin Edisen
Fishery

Mount
Ojibway
Tower

Ransom Hill

Across the harbor from Three Mile Campground is the site of the Johnson family fishing and tourist camp. The Davidson family purchased the camp and built a two-story colonial revival house in 1922. Their elegant summer home was an anomaly among the mostly unfinished interiors of Isle Royale's single-story summer cabins. After Isle Royale National Park was formed, the house hosted the Boreal Forest Research Station and visiting national park staff.

West of the Three Mile Campground, Rock Harbor narrows, in some places spanning less than a quarter mile. About 2 miles more, the shore dips into another shallow cove. Green shelter roofs punctuate the dark forest behind beach alders. You've arrived at Daisy Farm's long gravel beach.

Outer Islands

The day was bright and already warm when twelve-year-old Geneva, her bestie, Ava, and I woke at Three Mile Campground. As we crammed sleeping bags into stuff sacks and loaded gear into our kayaks, a familiar last day sadness enveloped me.

"Let's paddle the outside shores!"

The Isle Royale Queen ferry would not depart until 3:00 pm. We had plenty of time. Our boats were light and our arms strong from daily paddling. We glided a half mile across the harbor and paused for a moment to study breaking waves. We noted the deeper channel in the shoal between Outer Hill and Mott Islands, zipped through, and burst onto open Lake Superior. Rock streamed beneath our hulls. The Lake's enchanted timelessness swept away my heartache.

Stretched for a last sunbath on the baked gravel of a Smithwick Island beach, we devoured handfuls of almonds until the long, low tones of the Isle Royale Queen's horn rippled over the water. Ahead of us lay unloading our boats and arranging duffel bags, boats, and paddles on the dock for loading. It was time to slip onto the water and follow the Queen into the harbor.

You'd think the water rutted, the way boats heading southwest from the marina cling to Rock Harbor. But when conditions are right, paddling out Smithwick Channel and along the outer shores of the chain of islands defining Rock Harbor's southeastern edge offers solitude and a ride on Lake Superior's swells. On a clear day, ridges from Conglomerate Bay to Saginaw Point are a blue swipe across the southern horizon. Frequent cuts between islands allow you to soak in this expansive view with no great exposure.

Any fishing boats will be far off. Pocket beaches entice you to land and sunbath. Or comb their fine gravel for agate and turtle-backed chlorastrolite greenstones. Enjoy these stones and leave them for the next adventurer to find. Explore Lorelei Lane and other narrow water alleys between islands to experience a tranquil contrast to open Lake Superior's energy.

A white buoy off Mott Island's south shore marks the resting place of the *SS Algoma*. The *Algoma* left Owen Sound for Port Arthur on Thursday, October 5, 1885, with forty-five crew members, thirteen passengers, 134 tons of general merchandise, and 297 tons of railway supplies. Just through the Sault Saint Marie Canal, a storm turned Lake Superior into a wilderness of seething foam. The tempest howled and waves swept over the struggling steamer. A blinding snowstorm set in before morning.

"The passengers and crew were terrified beyond measure, and momentarily expected to see the steamer plunge to the bottom. By instructions of Capt. Moore, the officers circulated among the passengers, trying to allay their fears. They were panic stricken, however, and huddled together in the cabin, where the screams and prayers of the women and children could be heard above the thundering of the gale."–Saginaw Courier-Herald, 11/11/1885.

Hurricane-force winds rolled the ship so severely that the first mate ordered sails set to steady her. At 3 am a lookout was posted to sight the Passage Island Light. But she had drifted off course and ran aground off Mott Island at 4:40 am. Forty-eight persons drowned in the worst human life disaster in Lake Superior history.

Moskey Basin

Dawn came without a breath of wind. Mist threaded the high ridge behind the south shore, while bird wings whirred against the silence.

I'd watched a squadron of mergansers sweep the cove from my rock perch the night before, twelve brick red heads repeatedly dipping underwater. A loon's wild call rolled through the early evening from across the bay.

Three Sierra Club volunteers had arrived on Isle Royale that afternoon. In post-dinner twilight, they settled around me. Steeped in several days of solitude, I listened to their excited, talkative energy with the detached attention with which I'd watched the mergansers. I felt distant from both species.

Moskey Basin is a great spoon of water extending three miles southwest from Daisy Farm. The Scoville Point flow ridges the basin's north shore. Fault-jumbled hills of Portage Lake Volcanics rise above its south shore, protecting the basin from most winds. Kayakers often bypass Moskey Basin's extra 3.5 miles, leaving its shallow coves and ruffled shore all for you.

Hikes

Stoll Trail to Scoville Point

Stoll Memorial Trail to Scoville Point begins behind the Rock Harbor Lodge dining room. The 4.3-mile round-trip walk offers a chance to peer into native copper pits and the Smithwick Mine, operated by Captain Smithwick in the late 1840s. Numerous shafts were excavated to depths of ninety feet, but there are no records of copper production.

The trail follows a bluff overlooking Lake Superior. Expansive, wave-scoured rocks offer regular invitations to picnic, dip into the bracing water, or sit and listen to the surf.

Mount Franklin Trail

Beginning west of the Three Mile Campground, the Mount Franklin Trail is ten miles round trip from the Rock Harbor Trail. The trail crosses the quiet western end of the Tobin Harbor Trail and then crosses Tobin Creek before climbing two volcanic ridges. The top of the first ridge is an opportunity to view the rare columnar joints of the Edwards Island volcanic flow.

Between ridges, the trail drops into bogs edged with beaver-gnawed stumps. Attaining the Mount Franklin summit rewards you with a view of the thin blue line of Lake Superior's Canadian shore.

Mount Ojibway

Basalt was hot beneath my boots. I hopscotched between patches of naked stone, not wanting to crunch the crisp, silvery reindeer lichen. Aspen leaves flickered, but after paddling days of minding wind, on the trail I didn't care how hard it blew, or from which direction.

As I summitted the final ridge, Lake Superior's sapphire shimmer stretched from Amygdaloid Island to the gray blue of Canada's Sleeping Giant. An unimpeded breeze evaporated sweat from my shirt. A life-sized map of my route, from McCargoe Cove around Blake Point to Middle Island Passage, lay below.

Mount Ojibway, 1,133 feet above sea level, is a high point on the Greenstone volcanic ridge that spines Isle Royale from Mount Desor to Blake Point. The Mount Ojibway Trail dashes 1.7 miles from Daisy Farm Campground, climbs two ridges and drops to cross Tobin Creek and the marshes of Lake Ojibway before making the final 290-foot ascent. The Civilian Conservation Corps constructed a fire tower at this location in the 1930s. A steel structure replaced its deteriorating timber frame in the 1960s. Wrist-thick steel cables ground the metal against lightning strikes. The tower is no longer used to spot fires but serves as a national park communications mast.

Climb three stomach-dropping flights of steel steps for a view of the Canadian shore, Five Finger Bay, and a white speck: the Rock Harbor Lighthouse. The last flight of stairs and the tower's building are closed.

The 1.9-mile Daisy Farm Trail is an alternate path between the campground and the Greenstone Ridge Trail. It begins along Benson Creek and crosses boardwalks over two inland marshes lush with skunk cabbage, ostrich-fern, and elegant white bog orchids. The Mount Ojibway, Greenstone Ridge, and Daisy Farm Trails together make a worthwhile 5.5-mile loop hike.

For a 10.7-mile loop hike, climb the Mount Ojibway Trail and proceed northeast from the lookout tower along Greenstone Ridge Trail. Mount Franklin, another beautiful overlook point, is two and a half miles east from the tower. The Lane Cove and Mount Franklin Trail intersection is another 0.3 miles. Turn right and follow the Mount Franklin Trail along a bog, across Tobin Creek, and over one more ridge into the Three Mile Campground. From here, it is 4.2 miles back to Daisy Farm. Siskiwit Mine ruins lie along the Rock Harbor Trail about 1.7 miles southwest of its intersections with the Mount Franklin Trail.

Edisen Fishery

From the ridge behind the Daisy Farm Campground, sun's last rays bathed the whitewashed walls and salmon trim of the Edisen Fishery. I paddled across to investigate. A hand drill edged the net house door. Inside, knotted cotton strands and their smooth wooden floats draped from the ceiling. They'd not been wet in years, but the smell of linseed oil lingered. Inside the boathouse, I lifted a wooden door built into the floor over the fish well. Boat engines hung from a wall rail. Three boxes of worn shingles awaited the fire.

Isle Royale National Park maintains the Edisen Fishery as a demonstration of Isle Royale's commercial fishing history. Into the 1990s, Peter Edisen's red wooden net floats dotted Rock Harbor each morning. The Rock Harbor Lodge dining room served his daily catch each evening until his doctor said he was too old to lean over his boat's gunwales.

Edisen Fishery Dock House

Land your kayak on the gravel beach past the fishery's weathered boathouse and climb out beside the *Belle*'s large wooden hull. Built in 1928, the *Belle* was one of Isle Royale's earliest gas boats. Arnold Johnson hauled out here in 1951 when he decided fishing didn't pay a living wage. He earned more as an Isle Royale resort visitors' guide.

Respect the privacy of volunteer camp hosts who inhabit the original fishing family home during the summer months. But you are welcome to step inside the net house and run your fingers through knotted cotton strings. Handle roughly fashioned knives laid on a rough wood table beneath the window. Nestled higher on the hill above the boathouse are two smaller cabins, built for the fish camp hired men. Peer through the door at a single-room, barely larger than the narrow bed beneath a hand-stitched quilt.

Rock Harbor Lighthouse

A quarter-mile loop trail links Edisen Fishery to the Rock Harbor Lighthouse. Near the end of the trail, a waist-high capstan nestles among thimbleberry bushes.

The Rock Harbor Lighthouse was the first to be built and is the only one of four Isle Royale lighthouses that no longer flings its beacon into the night. The fifty-foot brick tower and an attached house, completed in 1855, marked Middle Island Passage for vessels arriving to the Ransom copper mine with supplies. Its fixed white light was visible for fourteen miles.

As Isle Royale mining activity faded, so did the need for this light. It was extinguished in 1859, briefly rekindled in 1874 to serve a mining surge, and permanently quenched in 1879. Commercial fishers Arnold and Milford Johnson occupied the home from 1928 until the National Park was established in 1939.

When the Johnson fishers left, the lighthouse was unoccupied for several years until the National Park restored it as a shipwreck museum. Inside, a red-rimmed dinner plate and side dish emblazoned with the SS *George M. Cox* seal and leather shoes retrieved from the *Algonquin* sit behind glass. Shipwreck stories, enlarged from the newspapers of their day, spin on large prisms.

Climb the blue wood steps of the light tower's spiral staircase. The final ladder pops you through a hatch into the lightroom. Old glass warps a view of Middle Island Passage rock and water.

Rock Harbor Lighthouse

Wolf-Moose Study Basecamp

"The Wolves of Isle Royale walk a genetic tightrope suspended above extinction at the same time that the image of the wolf has become an icon of Isle Royale National Park."–Philip Scarpino, in Cultural Resources on Isle Royale National Park: An Historic Context

Moose Antler Garden at the Bangsund Cabin

A small sailboat floats on the cove across the harbor from Daisy Farm Campground. The Bangsund family ran a commercial fishing operation from here in the 1940s and 1950s. When Jack Bangsund died in 1959, the National Park Service allowed research ecologist David Mech to use the cabin as a base for summer field studies on the wolf-moose predator-prey relationship. Insulated from the rest of the world by Lake Superior's frigid water, Isle Royale was uniquely situated for such inquiry.

Before the Isle Royale study, similar predator-prey investigates only lasted a couple of years, the span of a single graduate student's research. When five years of wolf-moose data showed a compelling "balance of nature" relationship, ecologists suggested to Allen his study was finished.

Despite his detractors, Allen clung to Isle Royale's life and death drama of wolves and moose. More than a half century later, the study he began, currently led by Rolf Peterson, is the longest predator-prey study in the world.

Raspberry Island

A small wooden dock on Raspberry Island's Rock Harbor side provides access to a 1-mile loop trail. The trail wanders through the boreal forest and over bridges. An acidic bog beneath the low planks hosts carnivorous sundew and pitcher plants. Unless the blue *Sandy* occupies the dock, you'll likely have the island entirely to yourself.

Campgrounds

Below are campgrounds accessible for your Rock Harbor Gateway Journey.

Rock Harbor Campground

The Rock Harbor Campground is a couple hundred yards down a wide, rocky trail from the marina, the Visitor's Center, and seasonal access to a camp store, flush toilets, hot showers, laundry, trash, and recycling. It is conveniently located for dinner at the lodge dining room or the Greenstone Grill and evening ranger programs. An old-fashioned lodge gathering room with board games, books, and a porch overlooks Lake Superior.

Kayaks may be berthed above the Snug Harbor beach in front of the Greenstone Grill. There are also public racks near the Visitor's Center. You may borrow a wooden cart from behind the Visitor's Center to trundle your gear to one of twenty sites, including nine shelters. There is a potable water spigot along the trail. From June 1 to Labor Day, the Rock Harbor Campground stay limit is one night.

Tookers Island Campground

Beaufort scale-3 winds whistled through birch leaves and rustled spruce boughs. Breakers thundered on Tookers Island's outer beaches. Lee strolled to the dock and returned with a report on Rock Harbor conditions. "It's getting uglier out there. Mist and fog are settling in."

We left our tag on the shelter door handle and our gear strewn across its wooden floor. I hoped we would eventually climb into our dry suits and taste these waves. But Lee chose to read his Russian novel. I respect that. A book that keeps you happily shore-bound in inadvisable conditions is a recommended safety item.

Tookers Island is 1.5 miles across Rock Harbor from the marina. The dock is on the island's north shore. There are two shelters and no tent sites. The June 1 to Labor Day stay limit is three nights.

Tookers Island Campground is popular with motorboats, so it is often unavailable. Should you be lucky enough to find an empty shelter, there are two rock-cradled swimming beaches on the Island's Lake Superior side where you can soak up sunshine or take a brisk, private dip.

Three Mile Campground

Stormy weather had pinned our party for two days in the Rock Harbor Campground. When the waves finally calmed, we eagerly stowed gear into two kayaks and launched. An hour later, we looked up to see the wood walls and wide roof of a shelter nestled at the top of a sweep of glacier-polished basalt. We landed below the smooth curve of rock, carefully unloaded, and carried our boats and gear up the steep stone.

Sun pierced the cloud cover. From the warm rock, gazing across Rock Harbor and through the gap between Inner Hill and Mott Islands to the distant Lake Superior horizon, we'd arrived in paradise.

Three Mile Campground is 3 miles by trail and 2.5 miles by water from the Rock Harbor Marina. There are eight shelters, four tent sites, two docks, and a wide gravel beach. The June 1 to Labor Day stay limit is one night.

It is a bit of a climb from the gravel beach to the two shelters at the top of a round basalt knob with a water view. But if either of the shelters are available, the view is worth lugging gear up steep rock steps. On a sunny afternoon, the smooth curve of basalt under bare feet is warm. Silky headed river otters often troll the shore at dusk. A full moon will rise through the gap between Outer Hill and Mott Islands to splash quivering bands of gold across the harbor.

Caribou Campground

Cemetery Island Grave Marker

Caribou Campground is 5 miles southwest of the Rock Harbor Marina. The dock is on the island's north shore, tucked behind Cemetery Island. A shallow, sandy pocket behind the dock offers a perfect kayak landing. The June 1 to Labor Day stay limit is three nights.

There are two shelters and a tent site nestled into the meadow between them. This campground features lovely sunning and swimming beaches. You'll hear the gentle chime of the Middle Island Passage bell buoy. On clear days, the whitewashed walls and tower of the Rock Harbor Lighthouse glimmers from across Middle Island Passage. A fire ring and picnic table near the dock make an alfresco setting for conversations with your campground neighbors. Fishers may offer you some of their fresh catch.

Cemetery Island tucks into a notch in West Caribou Island's northwest shore. Make the short paddle and wander among grave markers, names barely readable on their weathered, lichen-draped wood. The graves date from the 1850s and commemorate Ransom and Siskiwit mine family members as wells as victims of the *Algoma* wreck. Caribou Campground provides convenient access to paddling Rock Harbor's outer shore islands.

Daisy Farm Campground

About 6 miles from Rock Harbor, kayakers arrive at Daisy Farm Campground on the long sweep of its narrow beach, which provides a gravel landing and driftwood seating for lakeside dining. A large pavilion with four picnic tables sits beneath the dim light of thick forest. There are sixteen shelters, six tent sites, and three group sites. The five shelters most convenient for paddlers nestle behind the beach's alder rim. The June 1 to Labor Day stay limit is three nights.

Set on the Ransom copper mine site at the intersections of the Rock Harbor, Daisy Farm, and Mount Ojibway Trails, Daisy Farm Campground is an Isle Royale crossroads. With prior arrangements, the *Voyager II* will pick up your party from its dock as part of its scheduled route. A park ranger has been stationed some summers in the small cabin west of the dock.

Moskey Basin Campground

Another 3 miles beyond Daisy Farm is the Moskey Basin Campground. This campground has six shelters, two tent sites, and two group sites. The June 1 to Labor Day stay limit is three nights.

Compared to the bustle of Daisy Farm, evenings are quiet at the Moskey Basin Campground. The water along the campground shore is usually warm enough by midsummer for a swim. Lake Richie is 1.3 miles. About 0.1 miles before its shore, a trail forks south to Chippewa Harbor, another 6 miles.

Onward

You've refined your kayaking and wilderness camping skills. You confidently pack your boat and launch and land on Isle Royale's stony beaches. A taste of open Lake Superior paddling along the southeast shores of Rock Harbor's outer islands has made you hungry for more.

The following chapter introduces a next level Isle Royale trip, from McCargoe Cove to Malone Bay. On this trip you will paddle Isle Royale's south shore, where no land blocks forty-five miles of Lake Superior fetch between you and Michigan's Keweenaw Peninsula.

The Middle Journey: McCargoe Cove to Malone Bay

Even usually flat McCargoe Cove was bumpy. We exited the cove and encountered three-foot rolling swells. Watching them slide beneath the Voyager II's bow, I'd been hungry to taste them with my paddle, and here they were, an entire lake of dynamic water!

The Rock Harbor Gateway Journey is a satisfying sample of Isle Royale, but there's so much more! A Middle Journey from McCargoe Cove to Malone Bay layers remote shores, agate beaches, and the thrill of rounding Hill, Locke, Blake, and Saginaw Points onto Rock Harbor's yummy history, hikes, and vistas.

The water distance from McCargoe Cove to Malone Bay is 43 miles, a distance you might paddle in three to five days. But the trip could also easily occupy ten. I've spent nineteen engaged paddling and hiking days on this route as out-and-back trips from Rock Harbor.

If a Minnesota launch is convenient, the *Voyager II* ferry will drop your party at McCargoe Cove Campground and pick you up from Malone Bay Campground. If a ferry from Houghton or Copper Harbor better fits your geography, you could do this trip as out-and-back paddles from Rock Harbor. A third option is to hire a water taxi.

This journey encompasses exposed conditions from the mouth of McCargoe Cove to Amygdaloid Channel, rounding Hill, Locke, and Blake Points, and the shore from Conglomerate Bay to Malone Bay. The longest reach with limited bailout options is 4 miles between Lea Cove and Chippewa Harbor.

Waves break over shoals extending beyond exposed points. Current and wave energy over these shoals generate confused conditions. Watch breaking waves for several minutes to identify a deeper channel and run through that or circle the farthest breaking water.

Parts of this route are remote. Don't count on nearby paddlers or motorboats for aid. Bring a VHF radio and listen to weather reports a couple of times each day and before setting out on any committed reach. Paddlers engaging this journey should have solid self- and assisted rescues. Either a wet or dry suit is recommended.

Arriving

Entering McCargoe Cove, the *Voyager II* will make a sharp turn past Hawk Island, and head directly toward the Cove's far shore. She'll weave like a drunken sailor as she navigates first right and then left, following the channel. If there have been waves, you'll notice the silence as you glide onto McCargoe Cove's narrow fjord.

McCargoe Cove Arrival

When your boats, paddles, and gear bags have been unloaded from the top of the *Voyager II* to the dock, you must decide whether to make your first camp here or begin your paddling journey. The Minong Copper Mine site is worthy of an afternoon visit. Whether your first night is here or elsewhere, a loon call across the twilit evening assures you you've escaped from your ordinary world.

Paddles

McCargoe Cove to Belle Isle

The morning dawned beneath a blanket of low clouds. McCargoe Cove, two miles deep and sheltered by ridges, offered no hint of Lake Superior's rough conditions.

We packed our gear into triangular dry bags and stuffed them into bows and sterns. A red bag large enough to engulf a small child was strapped to the stern deck of David's boat. Its twin was piled onto the deck behind me. Twelve-year-old Eamon's boat was light and his deck clear as we pushed off from McCargo Cove Campground's curved basalt and headed for Belle Isle.

Geneva was eight. She and I shared an Aquaterra Gemini, a kayak with a single cockpit encompassing both seats and an open hull from bow to stern. We strained to move our heavy load. Approaching Lake Superior's open water, all three boats paused in Birch Island's lee to don nylon spray skirts. The Gemini's five feet of skirt came in two parts and fastened between us with a long Velcro strip. We looped straps over our shoulders and tucked its bungeed edges beneath the cockpit coaming. We'd soon discover its limits.

Sealed into our boats, we paddled toward shoals at the cove's mouth. David and Eamon stayed in the channel. I nervously hugged the shore. But I realized my mistake when a Lake Superior wave broke over the shallow bottom and dumped water onto our spray skirt and into our boat. Not stopping to bail; we followed Eamon and David onto the open lake.

A northwest wind drove two-foot waves with whitecaps. Against an endless sea, David and Eamon's boats were miniature. Even flooded, I felt confident Geneva and I would manage our beamy barge. But what if David or Eamon capsized? Against the wind, I was not even sure we'd reach them, never mind effect a rescue.

My mind churned with calculated contingencies. Two miles of open Lake Superior lay between our position and Amygdaloid Channel's entrance. But Round Island sat in the middle of our route. I paddled close enough to David to shout.

"Let's land in that island's lee!"

It felt like forever before we slipped behind the island onto flat water. Tugging our boats onto a skinny strip of gravel, we celebrated safety with wide grins and granola bars. From Round Island we paddled into Herring

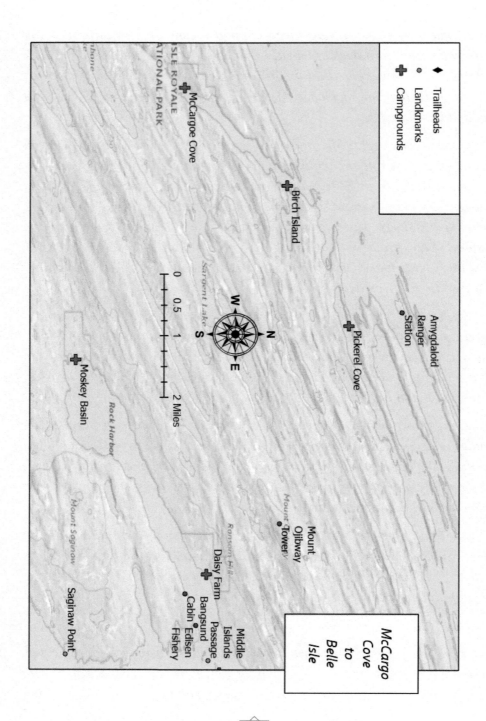

McCargo
Cove
to
Belle
Isle

Trailheads
Landkmarks
Campgrounds

ISLE ROYALE
NATIONAL PARK

McCargoe Cove

Birch Island

Sargent Lake

Amygdaloid
Ranger
Station

Pickerel Cove

0 0.5 1 2 Miles

Moskey Basin

Rock Harbor

Mount Saginaw

Saginaw Point

Mount
Ojibway

Mount Tower

Ransom Hill

Daisy Farm

Middle
Islands
Passage

Bangsund
Cabin Edisen
Fishery

Bay in the lee provided by its narrow 200 yards. With a short, easy portage from Herring into Pickerel Cove, the rest of our route to Belle Isle was protected.

It's time to stow your gear and slide your kayak onto McCargoe Cove. As you glide over its quiet water, you follow a fault line that crosses Isle Royale into Siskiwit Bay. Stanley Ridge to the east and Minong Ridge to the west frame its mouth. Just past Birch Island, zigzag through a geologic keyhole and paddle onto the full and uninterrupted power of Lake Superior.

From the mouth of McCargoe Cove, the Amygdaloid Channel entrance lies on a heading of thirty degrees. Depending on conditions, you might either enter the channel or paddle Amygdaloid Island's north shore, which traces Isle Royale's oldest volcanic flow. Billion-year-old magma bubbles sculpt cavities into vertical basalt. Water glugs from fairy-sized caves. The shore is four exposed miles with few landing options before you slip between Amygdaloid and Captain Kidd Islands.

Paddling the more protected Amygdaloid Channel, you will pass a ranger station near the island's southwest tip. Park housing at this location was renovated in 2015, and Belle Isle's volunteer hosts, David and Sarah Trigg, now make their summer home there. Two miles from the channel's entrance is a post marking the trailhead to the Amygdaloid Arch. Opposite the arch trailhead, a narrow keyhole separates Belle Isle and Isle Royale. Paddle through the keyhole and along Belle Isle's northwest shore or continue down Amygdaloid Channel another 1.6 miles.

Belle Isle's northeastern end is a narrow, alder-lipped crescent of polished pea gravel. An open-air pavilion peeks above a field studded with fireweed, strawberry, and raspberry bushes. Tucked between the grasses is a concrete shuffleboard, a remnant of Belle Isle's bygone grand resort days. There are two shelters at each edge of this meadow and several in the woods. Whether you are here for a lunch break, a leisurely afternoon, or to camp for a couple of days, Belle Isle Campground has enticing secrets to share with you.

McCargoe Cove to Belle Isle through Pickerel Cove

Isle Royale's predominant southwest winds can create bumpy lake conditions in Amygdaloid Channel. An alternate route is to make the short portage into Pickerel Cove. Commercial fishers rolled herring barrels along this easy 0.1-mile portage to waiting ships in Herring Bay. The protected route through Pickerel Cove, Robinson Bay, and Belle Harbor weaves among islands fringed with alder, western cedar, and dark basalt rock. The dock on Belle Isle's south shore is not your ideal landing location. Continue east and round the point to land on the beach nestled between two points on Belle Isle's northeast end.

Crystal Cove

Remnants of George McGrath's 1920s summer home on the east end of Amygdaloid Island are a half-mile paddle from Belle Isle. Paddle past the shoal extending from Amygdaloid Island's southern shore and its green roof and weathered gray walls are barely visible above the rocky shore. As you turn into Crystal Cove's fjord, fractured rock slabs and rock-filled dock cribs are visible through the

Crystal Cove Home

clear water. Pull your boat onto shore behind the dock and grab your camera, bug net, and lunch box.

The large log cabin featured indoor plumbing. A generator installed in a small building seventy feet from the house supplied electricity. Crystal Cove's dock accommodated the *America* as well as McGrath's 110-foot private yacht.

After the National Park Service purchased the site in the late 1930s, it remained unoccupied until the Park Service allowed Milford and Myrtle Johnson to move their fishing operation here from Star Island in 1956. The Johnsons fished the McCargoe Cove mouth, Steamboat Island, Five Finger Bay, and Todd Harbor until they retired in the 1980s. In the last few years, the Johnson's grandson, Steve Johnson, has returned from his Wyoming home to patch the roof and repair buildings.

A carved tree trunk with a wood nose and twisted coat-hanger glasses looms out of the dark woods. Drying reels draped with tattered net string, and a boat hauled out many seasons ago line the shore. A shed, its roof mostly caved, harbors a history of Crystal Cove laundry technology: tubs and scrub boards. The maple rollers of a wringer washing machine are still sound. Peer through dusty glass at an oak-framed treadle sewing machine. Each artifact whispers of a simpler time not so long ago, yet distant from our modern world.

Coat Hanger Glasses

Captain Kidd Island

Captain Kidd Island's western tip is less than 0.5-miles northeast of Amygdaloid. Paddle either its exposed northwest-facing cliffs, or a more protected route along the island's south shore. A small harbor with two docks lies at its northeast end.

Wayne and Marjorie McPherren purchased the 20.6-acre Captain Kidd Island in 1934 and constructed the log cabin cottage and boathouse. They sold the island to the National Park Service, retaining a life lease. The summer of 2007 was the last time Captain Kidd Island was occupied.

Admire the weathered gray wood of the compound constructed on this remote outpost. Take the short hike along the island's ridge to a white bench and a view of your campground on Belle Isle.

Belle Isle to Duncan Narrows Campground

The paddle from Belle Isle to Duncan Narrows is 9 miles. The route threads between Green and Dean Islands to Hill Point and the entrance to Five Finger Bay. If your schedule permits, explore some of the "finger" peninsulas and island shores. Five Finger Bay offers one of the best opportunities for wilderness solitude on Isle Royale's northeastern end.

When you've completed your exploration, head northeast around the swollen thumb of land that ends at Locke Point. Locke Point is the exposed northeast tip of the Minong basalt flow. The Minong flow traces southwest from your present location, forming the high ridge above McCargoe Cove Campground, the back wall of Todd Harbor, and one of the four slender rock fingers between the North Gap and McGinty Cove at Isle Royale's western end.

Beyond Locke Point, Minong's erosion-resistant basalt creates a long shoal. Unless conditions are flat, either paddle through a gap in the chaotic water, or around the buoy marking its end. Once around Locke Point, turn into Duncan Bay. Grace Island basalt flow on the north and the Greenstone flow on the south pinch Duncan Bay's entrance to create the Narrows.

Belle Isle to Duncan Narrows through Lane Cove

If lake conditions are rough, a protected route from Belle Isle to Duncan Narrows Campground is through Lane Cove, Stockly Bay, and Five Finger Bay. This route requires two short portages. A southeast heading from Belle Isle's eastern point takes you through a maze of islets into the mouth of Lane Cove. Inside the cove, scout for a portage route post near the northeastern end of its far shore. This flat portage is 0.1 miles.

The end of the portage places you on Stockly Bay's north shore. Paddle northeast. In 2 miles, Stockly Bay widens into Five Finger Bay. If your schedule allows, explore the islands of this remote and rarely paddled wilderness.

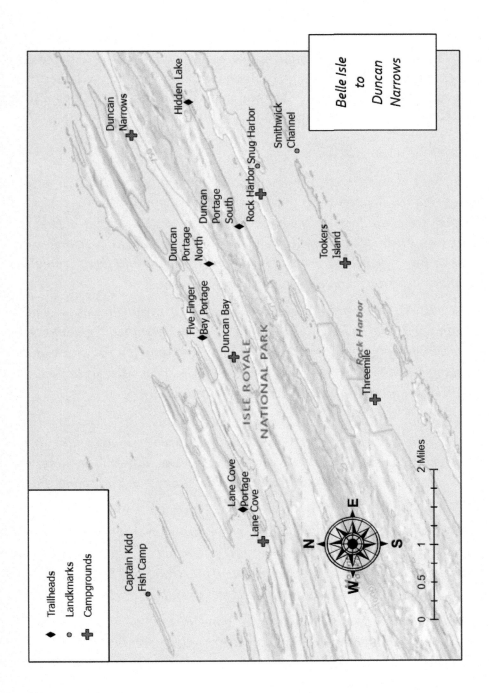

Captain Kidd
Fish Camp

Lane Cove
Portage
Lane Cove

Duncan
Portage
North

Five Finger
Bay Portage
Duncan Bay

Duncan
Narrows

Hidden Lake

Duncan
Portage
South

Rock Harbor Snug Harbor

Smithwick
Channel

Tookers
Island

ISLE ROYALE
NATIONAL PARK

Rock Harbor

Threemile

Trailheads
Landmarks
Campgrounds

Belle Isle
to
Duncan
Narrows

N
E
W
S

0   0.5   1   2 Miles

The second portage, 0.2-miles from Five Finger Bay into Duncan Bay, is south of a rock extension marking the end of Stockly Bay's south shore. The Duncan Bay Campground is less than a mile southeast from the portage's far end. Your chances of finding a campsite here are better than at the more popular Duncan Narrows camp. If you choose to try your luck at the Duncan Narrows Campground, it is another 2 miles northeast.

Rounding Blake Point

Garnet wiped the eastern horizon. Sleeping bags muffled our sleepy voices against the soft pit-pit of rain on mossy shingles as we discussed whether we should we roust ourselves to round Blake Point before the wind came up. Or we could spend the day paddling and hiking from Duncan Bay's protected water. The second choice would let us snuggle a few more luxurious moments in our warm cocoons.

A whoosh of air from the cracked valves of Elizabeth and Mohan's sleeping pads marked our choice to go. We quickly stuffed bags into their sacks and toted gear to our kayaks. Thirty minutes from the crack of the air mattress valves, we wiggled into neoprene spray skirts, slipped into life jackets, and tugged our boats onto the water.

The rain had stopped. Our boats rocked on a gentle, low-frequency swell. Under low clouds and with no wind, the water seemed oddly warm. Along the Palisades, a hundred vertical feet, we paddled close enough to touch their gleaming wet basalt. And then the Blake Point day marker rose from the naked rock ahead.

Still in the lee, only a rippling horizon hinted at what lay ahead. But as we approached Blake Point, the swell steepened. A following sea lifted our hulls on wave crests and dropped them into troughs. The chaotic shoal break ahead stretched several hundred feet past the storm-polished rock.

Adrenaline surged. Scanning for gaps in the foam—deeper areas where only the biggest waves broke, we pressed our feet firmly against our foot pedals and pulled on our paddle shafts. Our hips liquid against the choppy sea, we resolutely paddled through.

Blake Point

Blake Point is 8 miles from Belle Isle Campground and 3 miles from Duncan Narrows Campground. Approaching from Isle Royale's north shore, the last 0.75 miles are the Palisades. These vertical cliffs offer no landing. Once around the point, it is another half mile to Merritt Lane's protected water.

Blake Point is Isle Royale's last expression of the Greenstone lava flow before it plunges below the water to emerge briefly on Passage Island and vanish again beneath Lake Superior's surface. Blake Point's sharp ridge can create calm conditions on one side even when the other side seethes with rough water.

Rounding Blake Point from south to north, land at the Merritt Lane Campground and hike 0.6 miles to the point to inspect conditions on the other side. From Isle Royale's north shore, however, there is no scouting option. Your best bet is to pay careful attention to marine weather reports and to study the Lake Superior horizon for the rippling tell of bigger conditions.

Once around Blake Point, there are several paddling options into Rock Harbor. Regardless of Lake Superior's sea state, Merritt Lane, barely 300 feet wide, will be flat. Here, beneath cedars towering from its shore, the world is silent but for bird call and perhaps the gentle pit-pit-pit of rain. The 0.5-mile break between Merritt Lane and the equally tranquil Tobin Harbor, however, can be rough. If you reach the Rock Harbor Marina through Tobin Harbor, you will land at the seaplane dock and make a 0.25-mile asphalt sidewalk portage. Drag a cart from the Visitors' Center to trundle your gear.

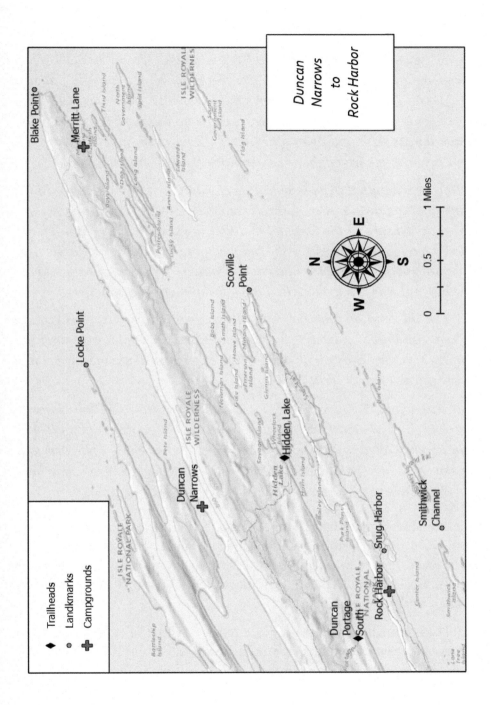

Duncan Narrows
to
Rock Harbor

Trailheads
Landmarks
Campgrounds

The water off Blake Point had been rough. Waves broke over a quarter-mile long shoal, stirring up a frothy mess. We happily paddled onto Merritt Lane's sheltered water. Of the two miles before us into Tobin Harbor, only a half mile was exposed, Once into the Harbor, a sentinel of islands across its mouth would protect us from Lake Superior waves. It didn't occur to me we might not make Rock Harbor that afternoon.

But, as we pulled from behind Porter Island, we were slammed by a twenty-knot headwind. A motorboat rounded Scoville Point, and headed toward us. Unsure of the channel location, we dropped back into Porter Island's lee to allow room for the bigger boat to maneuver. Passing us, the captain leaned out his window and shouted. His urgency was evident, but wind and waves battering Red Rock Point muffled his message.

When the boat had passed, we pulled again into the exposed gap. In different conditions, it would have been a short, ten-minute crossing. But we made slow headway against the wind. After several minutes, we called it and returned into Merritt Lane.

It was David Trigg's motorboat that had passed us in the channel. Now docked at Merritt Lane Campground, he'd organized our welcome. Eight hands waited at the shore, ready to grab our wrists and carry our boats over the algae-slick rock. Water was boiling for tea. Space had been cleared in the shelter for us to change.

The alternative to paddling Tobin Harbor is to weave among Porter and North Government Islands and then along the undulations of coves, shoals, and beaches that are Scoville Peninsula's south shore. Soon, you will come to Smithwick Channel. Turn north, pass the lifeboat memorial to the SS *America*, and enter Snug Harbor.

Rock Harbor might be your happy interlude of civilization, a chance to wash laundry and eat a hamburger cooked by someone else. You can study wooden signs with images of bygone resorts, supplement your provisions with convenience store purchases, catch an evening lecture on island ecology, or buy souvenirs. You can purchase tokens for a shower or rent a resort room with a bed and sheets.

If Rock Harbor Marina is an unwelcome intrusion into your wilderness experience, something to be passed through a quickly as possible, you might make a quick landing to toss your trash before scrambling back into your boat toward your next destination.

Rock Harbor to Middle Island Passage

The Gateway Rock Harbor Journey section describes these paddles.

Middle Island Passage to Chippewa Harbor

Quiet enveloped West Caribou Island. Middle Island Passage's bell buoy was silent, while yesterday's roar of surf against the outer beach had faded to a whisper. I slipped out of my sleeping bag, stashed gear into bags, hauled it to the beach, loaded the boat, and sealed hatches. I planned to paddle to Moskey Basin; a deep spoon of lake surrounded by ridges that blocked the wind.

Cedar clung to cracks in the cliff's wet basalt. Yesterday's raging waves now gently lapped the Middle Passage islands. Saginaw Point pierced the Lake Superior horizon. A ranger had warned me of conditions at Saginaw Point. "More people get in trouble at Saginaw Point than rounding Blake." Did I dare run this reach solo? As I pondered the question, my boat swung south. If I didn't run this route in these near perfect conditions, I never would.

The paddling distance from Middle Island Passage to Chippewa Harbor is 7 miles. Between the Passage and Saginaw Point, the shore offers protected landings, the last one being Lea Cove. Beyond Saginaw Point, the shoreline bends southwest. Other than bald eagles gliding the shore's edge and loons bobbing on the swell, you will probably paddle this stretch alone.

A shallow shelf extends about 300 feet from the shore. Under calm conditions, boulders invite rock gardening and offer regular landing

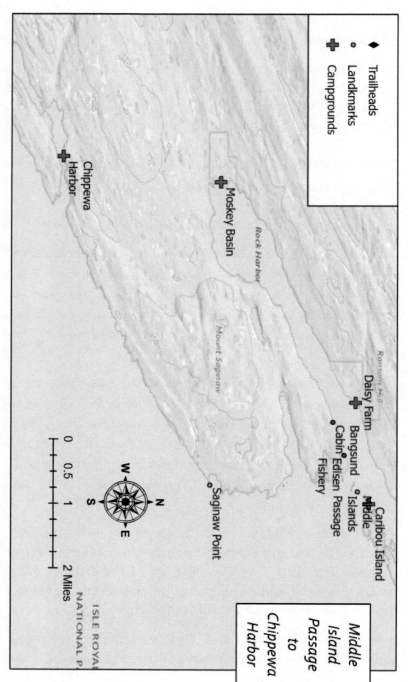

Middle Island Passage to Chippewa Harbor

Legend:
- ◆ Trailheads
- ○ Landkmarks
- ✚ Campgrounds

options.

In a heavy sea, however, you want to paddle offshore to avoid the chaos of breaking waves. Landing would be difficult or impossible.

Chippewa Harbor's opposite shore blends seamlessly with the near shore. As you approach, however, a white square navigational aide on the east bank marks the harbor's mouth. Just inside, black basalt plunges vertically to create a deep pool for the first quarter mile. As the entrance narrows, scan the right shore for the small cabin that was the Chippewa Harbor schoolhouse. The dock and campground will be on your right.

View from Chippewa Harbor School

Chippewa Harbor to Malone Bay

Meter-high waves, their tops level with my head, were an endless roller-coaster of effortless lift and drop. I paddled a course far from shore, beyond the long rock fingers where waves broke. Paddling the biggest waves yet shifted something within me. Apprehension regarding my demise, for better or worse, took a step back. I landed feeling happy and confident.

The ten-mile paddle from Chippewa Harbor to Malone Bay Campground has rocky shores, pocket beaches, and coves barely big enough to earn the

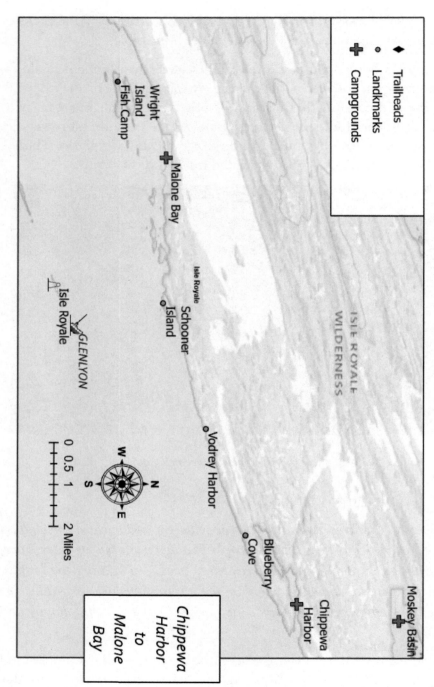

Trailheads

Landmarks

Campgrounds

Wright
Island
● Fish Camp

✚ Malone Bay

Isle Royale

Schooner
○ Island

Isle Royale
△ Isle Royale
GLENLYON

Vodrey Harbor ○

ISLE ROYALE
WILDERNESS

Blueberry
Cove ○

✚ Chippewa
Harbor

✚ Moskey Basin

W ─ N
S ─ E

0 0.5 1   2 Miles

*Chippewa
Harbor
to
Malone
Bay*

name

"harbor." One of them is Vodrey, named for the fisher who operated a camp from this shallow cove in the early 1900s. The Isle Royale Lighthouse on Menagerie Island pierces the horizon ahead. A shallow shoal between Isle Royale and Schooner Island is navigable for kayaks in all but the lowest Lake Superior levels. Once over the shoal, the 0.7-mile reach

between Schooner and the east end of Ross Island is exposed to wind or waves from the southeast. The direct route to the Malone Bay Campground is west, between Hat and Ross Islands and then slightly northwest.

Menagerie Island Paddle

With no dock or clear landing, I pulled my boat onto a narrow shingled beach behind a shallow basalt ledge. I clambered up the fifteen-foot cliff. Thick moss and lichen between bare stone suggested almost no one stops here. Walking across the unkept yard, I studied waves that licked the sloping basalt on the Lake Superior shore.

Isle Royale Lighthouse on Menagerie Island

From the Malone Bay Campground, Isle Royale Lighthouse is a white spire on the horizon. Sunset flames the red sandstone of the lightkeeper's house, just before the first flash of its reassuring beam. A paddle to this historic site is worth your time.

The distance from the Malone Bay Campground is 3.3 miles. Check the weather forecast and the horizon before launching. Winds from the east or west will kick up waves on the long fetch from either direction. Arriving at Menagerie, you can land in a small, rocky cove below the house. Other landings are on the island's western end.

Like the Rock Harbor Lighthouse, commercial copper mining impelled Isle Royale Lighthouse construction. In 1873, Congress appropriated $20,000 for a light to guide copper mine vessels toward the Island Mine, near the head of Siskiwit Bay. Its sixty-one-foot, double-walled octagonal tower of whitewashed sandstone was completed in 1875. The spacious keeper's dwelling is two floors of red sandstone housing eight rooms, five closets, and a brick chimney. Iron shutters protected the lowest windows from storm waves.

John Malone began keeping the Isle Royale Light in 1878. When told by his superintendent that a married man was needed, he promptly wedded Julia Shea. John and Julia lived on the island with their eleven children each year from May until December. The family collected a thousand gull eggs during each May's nesting season to supplement rations. Gulls have not forgotten that theft. They will sweep your boat if you paddle too close to their nests.

Between John and his son, Al, the Malone family kept the Isle Royale Light for thirty-one years. Logbooks provide a snapshot of the stormy weather they endured.

On October 16, 1880: "Hail, snow, and rain—a tempest; Lost boat, boathouse ways, and dock. It was impossible to save anything. I don't believe a cat could get from the dwelling to the boathouse. It hailed awful."

On November 10, 1884: "It is almost impossible for us to stay here much longer, for we have to cut the ice from the way every day or we could not launch our boat, the only hope we have of getting off for winter quarters."

On May 11, 1885: "Arrived here at 12 o'clock and commenced lighting up. We had to keep three stoves going night and day steady to heat up the house. It was just like an icehouse. The lake is full of ice, and the weather is very cold."

Relics of the lightkeeper's days include the two-story home, several outbuildings, and a long concrete sidewalk to the original boat dock. The orange, lichen-covered rocks of the island's south shore make a great walk or paddle.

The Filigree Ball

Beyond a small porch, bees hummed among pink rose blooms. Only a knotted cord through a hole in the door, not the usual heavy padlock, closed the Wright Island cabin. Disregarding a "no trespassing" sign, I went in.

A bit of light seeped past boarded windows. A cloth screen divided the living room from a small alcove with a tumble of clothing covering a wrought iron bed. From the bedside table flashed a gilded book title: The Filigree Ball.

I'd finished reading my only book the night before. I longed to tuck this one into my dry bag. No one would ever know. There were more modern titles on a living room shelf of planks and cinder blocks—paperbacks by Heinlein and Agatha Christie. But I had no right to be here. Like an addict passing on her next fix, I left them all.

Wright Island is a mile southwest of Malone Bay Campground. A string of islands formed from Copper Harbor Conglomerate defines Siskiwit Bay's north and south boundaries. One string extends from Schooner to Wright Islands.

Wright Island Fishing Boat

The other is the islands between Menagerie Island and Point Houghton. Wright Island's west shore was a Scandinavian immigrant fishing camp beginning in the 1890s. Sam Johnson came directly from Sweden to Isle

Royale in 1888. Sam's son, Steve Johnson, built Wright Island's log cabin in the mid-1920s. His daughter, Ingeborg Johnson Holte, spent eighty summers in that cabin. She fished from there with her husband, Ed Holte. Ed Holte was a valued Isle Royale gas-boat mechanic. When Ed died in 1971, Ingeborg continued the fishing business until 1980. Her last summer on the island was 1984.

Hikes

Minong Mine Hike

For at least four thousand years, Anishinaabe paddled from Lake Superior's north shore to the island they call Minong. McCargoe Cove's gash in Isle Royale's otherwise steep northern shore offered a natural landing spot. A two-mile line of Anishinaabe copper pits lies at the end of a short side trail that begins 0.8 miles from the McCargoe Cove Campground on the Minong Ridge Trail. Here, Anishinaabe opened ore veins by firing rock and quenching it with water. Using boulders to support the walls, they constructed drains to empty water from their copper pits.

Post-colonization copper prospecting at the Minong Mine began with a claim in 1872. The Minong Company accessed copper from open pits and two excavated shafts. One hundred and fifty miners arrived at the site each morning on a railroad from McCargoe Cove. A post office, dam, a stamp mill to crush ore, and a blacksmith's shop supported the miners, their families, and mining operations. Over 249 tons of copper, some nuggets as heavy as six tons, were commercially extracted from the Minong mine. After ten years of operation, it was abandoned in 1885, when the price of copper fell.

Anishinaabe pits, Minong Company pits (now filled with water), tailing piles, railroad tracks, and ore carts remain at the site. Shafts are unstable and dangerous. Do not enter them. Leave the artifacts where they are.

Amygdaloid Arch

A wooden post on Amygdaloid Island's south shore, 1.8 miles past its western end, marks the trailhead to Amygdaloid Arch. Land on the narrow beach, secure your boat, and follow a poorly marked path northeast to a relic sea arch framing Lake Superior. Sixty-five feet above the current water level, the ancestral Lake Nipissing sculpted the twelve-foot span. Climb the stone along the arch's left edge for a view of the Canadian shore and to gather blueberries from along the ridge trail, as people have done since ancient times.

The Duncan Portage

Jim, Patty and Niles were Minnesotans from the Twin Cities, with the thick blood of their Scandanavian ancestors and warm, puffy jackets they pulled from thimble-sized bags. We'd kayaked together to Captain Kidd Island, explored its relic buildings and caught a view of our Belle Isle camp from its high southern cliffs. We'd returned to the dock when Ranger Carl. wearing a neatly pressed park service shirt, gleaming badge, bill cap and strapped sunglasses, expertly landed his motorboat and stepped onto the planks.

"Have you heard tomorrow's weather forecast? It will be gale force winds and a small craft advisory."

"You're kidding us, right?"

Jim and I planned to kayak to Rock Harbor tomorrow, arriving in time for his scheduled ferry departure the next morning. But neither of us would be rounding Blake Point in gale force winds. Ranger Carl switched on his high-powered VHF radio so we could hear the forecast for ourselves.

Later that afternoon, after careful consideration and conversation, Jim and I had a plan. We'd launch early and try to round Blake Point before the predicted storm arrived. If we missed our weather window, we would drop into Duncan Bay and make the strenuous Duncan Portage.

That evening, Jim and I toted stoves and cooking gear to the Belle Isle pavilion. We brought a foil packet of Indian spinach paneer, masa for tortillas and home-made beef jerky. Onions, garlic, green peppers, and zucchini were fresh enough to be edible despite traveling for a couple of weeks in Jim's kayak. We'd cook dinner for the four of us. If portage turned out to be tomorrow's fate, food eaten that night would be less to haul.

Niles brought lake-chilled white wine. Patty dropped her headlamp into a Nalgene bottle to cast an elegant glow across the table. It was late and fog wrapped the meadow when we reluctantly said good night and headed to our separate camps. Niles promised to make Jim's morning coffee to speed our launch.

But it was not until 9 am, under a low gray sky and a light sprinkle of rain, when we floated our loaded boats from the pea gravel beach. Although the lake was flat, we were in a race against the forecasted storm. I settled into the fastest pace I could sustain for thirteen miles.

Conditions were perfect. We made good time. But just passed Dean Island a cool breeze bussed my cheek. The wind came up fast. Four miles later, a hundred yards of turbulent foam over Locke Point's shoal blocked our path. From behind me, came a sharp intake of breath. I did not like imagining a rescue in these shallow, chaotic conditions.

I studied the foam, searching for any consistent gap in the breaking waves. Once I had identified my spot, I focused on keeping my center of gravity low, and my momentum confident. Jim followed me through.

Once past Locke, we flew toward Blake Point, driven by wind and following seas. But it was just a few minutes before Jim's question rang over the water. "What do you think?"

No way did I want to turn and battle a headwind into Duncan Bay and then make the Duncan Portage. "I think we should go for it. We will be around Blake Point before conditions are much worse. Rounding Blake may be tricky, but as soon as we are on the other side, we'll be in the lee, with no worse conditions than these and quite likely better."

We paddled a few minutes when I heard Jim say, "I don't like this. I think we should bag it."

My heart sank. Nevertheless, without hesitation, I called back. "OK. Coming about."

If seas are too rough to round Blake Point, take a weather day. There is no reason to make the Duncan Portage with sea kayaks if you don't have to. It makes a lovely day hike without a boat on your shoulder or gear bags tugging from your elbow.

But a water taxi will not make the perilous journey on your behalf if conditions are too rough to kayak. So if your schedule does not allow you to wait for suitable weather, the Duncan Bay Portage might be your best option. And even from beneath a kayak hull, it is impossible not to appreciate the lush boreal forest enveloping this north-facing trail.

The portage begins on a sloping hillside with barely space to thread your boats and gear between the broad roots of northern white cedar. This steep north edge of the Portage Lake Volcanics lava flow is wetter than its southeast-facing slope. The first half mile is a narrow, steep ascent between shoulder-high rock carpeted with sphagnum moss. The trail is dark beneath a thick canopy of birch, fir, and spruce.

At the top of the Greenstone Ridge, 180 feet higher than the Lake Superior shore, the trail opens onto a flat meadow surrounding the Greenstone Ridge Trail intersection. From this summit, the portage continues another 0.5 miles across a roller-coaster of resistant pyroclastic Portage Lake Volcanic flows. Between each ridge, the trail drops into marshes, some crossed on a boardwalk. The portage ends at Tobin Harbor, 0.5-miles west of the dock and a 0.25-mile asphalt trail to Rock Harbor.

Ishpeming Trail

It had been more than a week since my last shower. On Lake Siskiwit's shore, I stripped out of my clothes and rubbed my legs, toes, feet, shoulders, face, neck, and armpits with handfuls of fine sand. A bracing rinse left my skin smooth and clean.

My freshly washed state inspired several minutes of contentment. But too soon, nagging questions penetrated my bliss. What was I doing here? How did this wilderness paddling serve my life's purpose? At home, busyness smothered these questions. But wilderness's expansive solitude allowed no escape.

Having no answers, I turned to lunch: crackers topped with sausage and squares of soft, almost-melted cheese. Once sated, I had more insight. The pulse of paddle strokes and hiking steps, the rhythm of making and breaking camp regulated my days. Dawn woke me. Darkness signaled time to slither into my sleeping bag. I was practicing slowness; practicing life free of the bondage of calendars and clocks.

The trail from Malone Bay Campground to Ishpeming Tower on the Greenstone Ridge is 7 miles. The first 0.3 miles traces the Siskiwit River from Malone Bay to Siskiwit Lake. Even if you go no farther, this short hike offers a chance to swim in Siskiwit Lake's warmer water.

The Ishpeming Trail continues west along a ridge above the Siskiwit Lake shore before dropping to cross a marsh at the lake's west end. The trail then climbs both the Scoville Point and Tobin Harbor volcanic flow ridges before a final ascent to the top of the Greenstone Ridge flow and the Ishpeming Fire Tower. Trees have grown to block any view from the tower.

Campgrounds

Paddlers on the Middle Journey route are required to occupy Isle Royale National Park's designated campsites. You might spend days on the water and see no one, but unless you come before July or after Labor Day, your campground will likely host paddling, motorboat, sailboat, or hiking groups in addition to yours.

McCargoe Cove Campground

McCargoe Cove Campground is located 2 miles from open Lake Superior. The campground has six shelters, three tent sites, and three group sites. The

June 1 to Labor Day stay limit is three nights. With prior arrangements, the *Voyager II* will drop your party at the campground dock as part of its scheduled route.

Anishinaabe copper mine pits and artifacts, and the 1870s Minong Mine are located 1.3 miles from the McCargoe Cove Campground along the Minong Ridge Trail. The Greenstone Ridge Trail is 3.1 miles from the campground on the Indian Portage Trail.

Belle Isle Sunrise

Birch Island Campground

Birch Island sits inside McCargoe Cove's mouth. There is one shelter, often occupied by motorboats, and a single tent site. The June 1 to Labor Day stay limit is three nights.

Captain Robert Francis built a log cabin on Birch Island in the early 1920s. Tchi-ki-wis and her husband, John Linklater, inhabited the cabin in the 1920s and 1930s. They were the last native people to live on Isle Royale. Timothy Cochrane, National Park Service backcountry ranger and historian, observed, when the National Park Service burned their cabin in the 1970s, the *"last material remnant of an Ojibwe home on Minong was gone."*

Belle Isle Campground

Stars in the June morning sky began to wink out before 5 am. I'd lifted my boat from its nest on the meadow and laid it at the water's edge. I'd packed everything but a cup of granola when Joe approached, carrying his five-gallon bucket and a small foam pad.

"Shall we watch the sunrise?"

I followed him to the precise spot where the sun would glow orange through a gap between Belle Isle and an island off her northeast point. Silence marked the sun's slow ascent. A few minutes later, I snapped my spray skirt around the cockpit coaming and dipped my blade to begin the twenty-mile paddle to Little Todd Harbor.

Belle Isle has welcomed Isle Royale visitors for more than a century. The Belle Isle Resort opened in 1912. Compared to guest houses retrofitted into rustic commercial fishing cabins, its oriental rugs and walls decorated with fish trophies were luxurious. A fieldstone fireplace warmed its main lodge. Its two bathhouses featured toilets and electric lights. Each morning staff delivered hot water to twenty-eight cabins. Guests slammed golf balls across a nine-hole course. There was tennis and a concrete shuffleboard. A walled-off corner of Lake Superior was deemed the "swimming pool."

Of the original resort buildings, only a hipped-roof, wooden-framed guest cottage remains. But visitors can still climb narrow, hundred-year-old concrete steps between Shelter #6 and tent site #10 for a view from the isle's southeast point.

Belle Isle Resort Stairs

Of the six shelters, the two nearest the gravel beach are the most convenient for paddlers. A pavilion with a fireplace, a large grill, and picnic tables can host all Belle Isle visitors. The small pea gravel beach with a view toward Steamship Rock invites long conversations or time with your journal or sketchbook. On the beach at twilight, bats may fly over your head, hunting for mosquitoes drawn by your breath. The June 1 to Labor Day stay limit is five nights.

Lane Cove Campground

Lane Cove Campground is at the end of the Lane Cove Trail. A 2.4-mile hike from the Greenstone Trail, the campground's five tent sites may be occupied by hikers as well as paddlers. The June 1 to Labor Day stay limit is three nights.

Pickerel Cove Campground

Pickerel Cove, with neither a trail or dock, is accessible only by canoe or kayak. It has a single tent site, guaranteeing solitude. The June 1 to Labor Day stay limit is two nights.

Duncan Narrows Campground

Rain pounded the lake's dark surface in a chaotic roar. Each of thousands of drops hesitated for one glittering moment before melting into the water. The Duncan Narrows Campground dock, barely visible in the gloaming, was empty. A single kayak snuggled under the shore alders. I landed on a sand beach, popped my spray skirt, and quickly tugged gear from hatches.

A figure swaddled in rain garb appeared from around the shelter wall. "Do you need a hand?"

My response was reflexive. "No, thanks. I've got this."

What would have been the harm in allowing someone to help haul my gear into the shelter before everything was soaked? Fifteen solo days had not improved my social skills.

As darkness had settled, this stranger probably expected to enjoy a solitary campground. I tried to be more friendly.

"Sorry to intrude."

"That's okay. You are headed west, and I am headed east."

"I'm not headed anywhere. I'm staying here tonight."

"I mean, our shelters face opposite directions." With that, he vanished

behind the shelter wall. For the rest of the night, the only sound was the pit-pit of rain.

The Duncan Narrows Campground is on the bay's south shore. The best landing is a ribbon of sand behind the dock. There are two shelters. The sunrise view through the Narrows from the east-facing shelter is an Isle Royale visitor favorite. The June 1 to Labor Day stay limit is three nights.

Duncan Bay Campground

Duncan Bay Campground, on the west end of Duncan Bay, is 2.4 miles southwest of the Duncan Narrows Campground. It can be accessed either through Duncan Bay, or with a short portage and a 0.4-mile southwest paddle, from Five Finger Bay. The campground has two shelters and one tent site. The June 1 to Labor Day stay limit is three nights.

Merritt Lane Campground

Merritt Lane Campground sits near Isle Royale's northeast end, 0.7 miles southwest of Blake Point. Kayakers from Rock Harbor often make this campground a base from which to observe lake conditions and wait for a weather window in which they can safely round Blake Point.

The Merritt Lane kayak landing is glacier-polished basalt just east of the boat dock. Beware the slippery footing. Berth your boats on the meadow above the rock. There is a single shelter and one tent site. The June 1 to Labor Day stay limit is three nights.

Campgrounds Between Merritt Lane and Chippewa Harbor

The Gateway Journey section describes these campgrounds.

Chippewa Harbor Campground

I lugged my plump, 10-liter water bag up the curve of worn basalt and stirred dehydrated beans into some of the filtered water. I sliced sharp cheddar, and spooned masa into a steel cup, added French gris salt and a couple of tablespoons of warm water, patted a thick tortilla, and laid it into sizzling olive oil.

Later, dishes washed, bedroll laid out, and food and gear stored for the night, I wandered back to the shore. Lake Superior was unusually low. A wide rock shelf, normally submerged, pierced the black water. A full moon, ascending through the dark basalt of the harbor's mouth, splashed a wavering golden path.

After a string of nights in which I crawled into my sleeping bag as daylight faded, 11 pm was late. But I'd be packed and paddling early the next morning, before wind built to toss waves against tomorrow's exposed shore.

Fishing Boat on Chippewa Harbor Shore

The Chippewa Harbor Campground offers four shelters, two tent sites, and one group site. Kayakers can expect to share the campground with sail and motorboats, as well as backpackers. The June 1 to Labor Day stay limit is three nights.

Chippewa Harbor water is often warm enough to swim. Trails from the campground lead to Lake Mason, 0.6 miles, and Lake Richie, 2.3 miles via the Indian Portage Trail. With prior arrangement, the *Voyager II* will pick up or drop off your party at Chippewa Harbor Campground dock as part of its scheduled route.

Malone Bay Campground

In the last moments of waning light, I filled a water bottle, placed it near the clothing bundle that served as my pillow, popped a bite of crystallized ginger into my mouth, brushed my teeth, and crawled into my sleeping bag.

Awaiting sleep, tomorrow's sea state was a regular preoccupation. I listened obsessively to water as it glugged against the back wall of a rock-worn chamber; to waves swooshing over the red stone beach. Were conditions building? Would tomorrow bring huge waves and impossible landings? Capsize and death?

Across three miles of water, the Isle Royale Lighthouse on Menagerie Island blazed in the setting sun. Deepening twilight silhouetted its tower against an indigo sky. Then, the evening's first flash of a six-second pulse pierced the darkness. Sensing a protective lineage that guided generations of ships to safety, I drifted into a peaceful, dreamless sleep.

The Malone Bay Campground is on the north shore of Malone Bay, a watery nub off the larger Siskiwit Bay defined by Hat, Ross, Malone, Channel, and Wright Islands. The campground is 0.5 miles west of the dock, behind a red gravel beach and a wide slab of weathered basalt. There are five shelters and two group sites. The June 1 to Labor Day stay limit is three nights.

A one-room log cabin squats beneath the forest behind the boat dock. Stocked with maps, historic photographs, and a book or two, its door is always unlocked. National Park Service staff housing, storage barns, and a communication tower are 0.1 miles north of the dock. In recent years, however, there has been no park ranger stationed here. With prior arrangement, the *Voyager II* will pick up or drop off your party at Malone Bay dock as part of its scheduled route.

Onward

I paddled Isle Royale for twenty-four years before I circumnavigated. If I'd known what I'm going to tell you in the next chapter, I'd have done it sooner.

The Committed Circumnavigation Journey

There is magic in circumnavigating Isle Royale; in wrapping around the entire Island and tasting every shore. You'll still miss things. Almost no one tucks into Brady Cove, adds ten miles to visit Siskiwit Bay's west end, or skirts Steamship Island's outer shore. But you'll see the Island from every direction.

Circumnavigation includes paddling shores exposed to long fetches and potentially large waves. Between the North Gap out of Washington Harbor and Huginnin Cove is a 4-mile paddle with limited or no landings. Beyond Huginnin Cove, 11.6 miles of Isle Royale's northwest shore to Thomsonite Beach has only a few steep beaches of polished cobble at the back of narrow faults in steep rock. These notch beaches offer landings on calm seas. In rough conditions, however, landing here would be difficult or impossible. There are no landing options for 3 miles between Little Todd Harbor and Wilson Point.

You'll be more isolated on a circumnavigation journey. Other than in Washington Harbor, it's rare to see another kayaker between Malone Bay and McCargoe Cove. There are fewer hikers on Isle Royale's western trails, which only rarely access the Lake Superior shore.

On preceding journeys, you might paddle solitary days, but park regulations required you to spend each evening in a designated campground. Unless you paddle thirty-two miles from Siskiwit Bay Campground to Grace Island in a single day, however, this journey will include at least one backcountry camp.

You can begin a Circumnavigation Journey at either Rock Harbor or Windigo and round Isle Royale clockwise or counterclockwise. Most paddlers circumnavigate Isle Royale clockwise. Winds blow from all directions, but predominantly from the southwest. Navigating the 11.5-mile reach between Huginnin and Little Todd Harbor, with a cliff shore and few to no landings, is faster with a tailwind. On the other hand, David Trigg, the Belle Isle park volunteer, has paddled Isle Royale for years and swears that Lake Superior currents favor a counterclockwise circumnavigation.

Having circumnavigated in both directions, my vote is clockwise. The paddling and hiking sections below assume clockwise circumnavigation beginning at Rock Harbor. But if you are beginning your circumnavigation from the equally suitable Windigo, simply pick up the route discussion in the middle and finish with the first section.

The Gateway Rock Harbor and Middle Journeys describe paddling, hikes, and campgrounds from McCargoe Cove to Malone Bay. This chapter describes the paddles, hikes, and campgrounds from Malone Bay Campground to McCargoe Cove.

Paddles

Malone Bay Campground to Point Houghton

As we paddled Siskiwit Bay's north edge, bruised purple clouds towered above the ridge ahead. Rather than crossing long reaches from point to point, we hugged the shore. Cedar perfumed the wet air. Responding to the shallow bottom, each swell surged under our hulls. If the storm broke, we had landing options.

One route from the Malone Bay Campground to Point Houghton is straight across Siskiwit Bay, 7.2 miles. If a southwest wind, however, kicks up waves and whitecaps on Siskiwit Bay's nine-mile fetch, a more conservative option is to paddle Siskiwit Bay's north shore to Hay Point and cross 2.7-miles from there to Point Houghton. The total distance of this route is 9.1 miles.

The most interesting route might be to paddle from the Malone Bay Campground southeast to Menagerie Island. See the Middle Journey for a description of Menagerie Island's paddle. From Menagerie island, head southwest along the Stone House, Long, Castle, Paul, and Redfin Island shores. This longer route, exposed to Lake Superior waves and wind, is 10.3 miles.

Point Houghton to Rainbow Cove

On a windless day and a flat sea, we flew along Isle Royale's southwest shore. Too soon, we passed the Head's distinctive, storm-polished conglomerate. We rounded Rainbow Point and rode into Rainbow Cove on the backs of easy swells. Lake Superior was lower than usual. Carrying three kayaks up forty feet of sliding pebbles left us breathless. We made dinner and set up camp.

To make space in my boat to provision our nineteen-day journey, I had traded my tent for a bivy sack and tarp. I fastened the high end of my tarp to alder branches and anchored its low corner with a stake into gravel. Snuggled beneath, no screen or nylon shielded my view. As night settled,

131

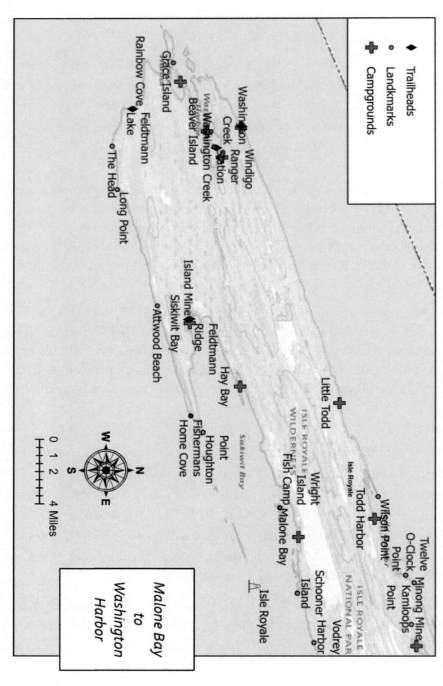

Map legend:
- ◆ Trailheads
- ○ Landmarks
- ✚ Campgrounds

Labels (south shore, bottom):
Twelve O-Clock Point
Minong Mine
Kamloops
Point

ISLE ROYALE NATIONAL PARK

Wilson Point
Todd Harbor
Isle Royale
Vodrey
Schooner Harbor
Island

Wright
ISLE ROYALE WILDERNESS
ISLE ROYALE ISLAND

Little Todd
Fish Camp
Malone Bay

Isle Royale

Labels (interior/north shore):
Washington Ranger Station
Windigo
Washington Creek
West Washington Creek Harbor
Beaver Island
Grace Island
Rainbow Cove
Feldtmann Lake
The Head
Long Point

Siskiwit Bay
Island Mine
Feldtmann Ridge
Hay Bay
Point
Houghton
Fishermans Home Cove
Attwood Beach
Siskiwit Bay

Compass: N W S E

0 1 2 4 Miles

Title block:

Malone Bay to Washington Harbor

132

lightning silhouetted black clouds over Minnesota's North Shore.

Hours later, I woke from a sound sleep to a wind's wild rush and the first drops of rain on the tarp. The next gust pulled a stake from the pebbles. The tarp corner lashed as if a storm dragon worried its toy. Crawling out, I grabbed a flying end of p-cord, wrapped it around a foot-long piece of driftwood, scooped a hole in the gravel and buried it, mounding more gravel over my anchor. Crawling back under what I hoped was a now secured tarp, I dried my wet skin and slipped into my sleeping bag. In the morning, we awoke to a glittering, storm-washed world.

Point Houghton to Rainbow Cove is 16.5 miles. Although you could paddle that distance in a single day, several beaches invite a picnic or a wild camp in the forest behind.

Southwest of Point Houghton, Fishermans Home Cove cuts a slash into the Houghton Ridge. Edward Seglem established one of Isle Royale's earliest commercial fisheries here in the 1890s. By the 1930s, the Rude family shared the complex with the Seglems. The site includes a residence, guesthouse, fish house, net house, helper's quarters, privy, tool shed, storeroom, net-drying reels, a smoker, and a sauna. The Rude family continues to occupy the site in summer months. Respect their privacy.

Once past Fishermans Home Cove, Isle Royale's shore is rock, punctuated by alluvial beaches. The Head, Long Point, and Rainbow Point are shaped from Copper Harbor Conglomerate. Where the conglomerate rock slips beneath the water along this shore, underwater reefs steepen Lake Superior waves. Named beaches include Little Boat Harbor, a mile southwest of Fishermans Home Cove, and Attwood Beach, another four miles.

Commercial Fishing Net Reel

Long Point lies 11 miles beyond Fishermans Home Cove. In the 1920s, Ingeborg Holte's fishing family waited here for the *America* to arrive and pick up their catch. The water was too shallow for the *America's* draft. Her family rowed their catch into deeper water and tossed fish from their boats into the maw of her massive hull. Holte remembers Long Point's elegant "uptown" house, built of native stone with a glassed-in front porch and hardwood flooring. The Long Point house and fishing camp were abandoned when the owners died and then torn down by the Park Service.

Landing on a beach west of the Head provides an opportunity to hike back and explore the overhang of this rock outcrop.

Rainbow Point to Washington Harbor

The distant end of the Scoville Point basalt flow protrudes into Grace Harbor a mile past Cumberland Point to form the Middle Point nub. Elizabeth, Mohan and I picked our way over a wide shelf of breadbox-sized stones, dimly visible in the twilight, to land and make camp. It never occurred to us that rough seas could pin us on its narrow beach.

I was shocked to wake the next morning to a 20-knot blow. Waves roared down the harbor. Nine lines of surf broke over rocks we had carefully navigated in flat conditions the night before. How could this happen? The map said "harbor," for heaven's sake.

I would have more than enough time to consider that and other questions. Could we launch and make our way to someplace more protected? Grace Island's lee shore and Washington Harbor were not a mile away. But getting into deeper water would be difficult. When the occasional yacht powered past us, its determined bow lifted toward the open lake, only to turn back onto protected water, we were even more reluctant to launch.

But the wind's barrage was maddening. We stacked stones and driftwood to shepherd the flame beneath our pot. Our beach, not fifteen feet wide when we landed, shrunk under the pounding waves. We considered options for a higher camp. But the wood behind was a bog of fallen logs. Any step might be onto solid ground or into a hole masked beneath a moss blanket.

Time was endless. We cooked a salve of afternoon tea and scones against the incessantly irritating roar. We paced a couple hundred feet along a narrow rim of dry stone. Photographed sculptures of stone and wood. Stared into the onslaught of waves.

After seventy-two relentless hours, at 6 pm the wind direction shifted slightly. The next morning, surf still broke over the Middle Point shoal. But one narrow water window might provide a path through the messy water. We walked along a couple hundred feet of shore, scanning for a better launch. But nothing was worth hauling our gear and boats.

We loaded boats, worked together to drop them into a deeper pool beyond the shore break, snapped our spray skirts and headed slightly west of north. We were beam to wave and wind as we crossed toward the narrow neck of Washington Island. But once tucked into the lee, we easily turned east and paddled along Grace Island's black basalt cliffs.

The opposite end of Isle Royale's Blake Point, with its sharp thrust into Lake Superior, is a wide sweep of gravel between Rainbow and Cumberland Points. Rainbow Cove is 3 miles along its shore and 2.4 miles straight across.

Rainbow Cove Sunset

A small stream and wood post mark the 0.5-mile Rainbow Cove Trail to Feldtmann Lake and the Feldtmann Lake Campground.

From the Feldtmann Lake trailhead in Rainbow Cove, the paddling distance to Windigo, at Washington Harbor's head, is 8.7 miles. Waves break over the shallow reef that extends beyond Cumberland Point. A buoy marks its end.

Grace Harbor connects Cumberland Point and Washington Harbor. Despite its harbor designation, the contraction between Washington Island and Middle Point focuses and concentrates westerly winds and waves. Grace Harbor sea conditions can be rough.

Washington Harbor

The Washington Harbor entrance lies between Card Point on the south and the North Gap. The Greenstone and Portage Volcanic lava flows mark its north and south shores. These ridges channel southwest winds.

The head of Washington Harbor is the mouth of Washington Creek and the Washington Creek Campground. The Windigo Ranger Station, Visitor Center, and camp store are on Washington Harbor's south shore, near its head.

West of the Washington Harbor mouth, paddling into the North Gap carries you over the *America* wreck. The affection of Isle Royale inhabitants for the *America* rings through the decades. Beginning in 1902, it plied a circuit from Duluth, Minnesota, around Isle Royale, and on to Thunder Bay. With twelve staterooms and a 1,200-passenger capacity, the SS *America* brought summer visitors to Isle Royale resorts.

The SS *America* was also a lifeline for commercial fishing and lightkeeper families. Each spring, they boarded with luggage and supplies. In the fall, they returned to spend winter months on Minnesota's North Shore. During otherwise isolated summer months, the *America* was their one touch with the larger world.

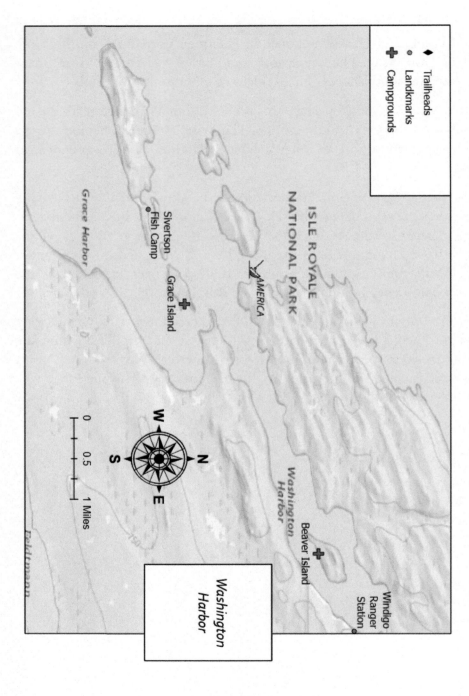

Washington
Harbor

ISLE ROYALE
NATIONAL PARK

Grace Harbor

Sivertson
Fish Camp

Grace Island

AMERICA

Washington
Harbor

Beaver Island

Windigo
Ranger
Station

Feldtmann

W N
S E
0   0.5   1 Miles

Trailheads
Landkmarks
Campgrounds

America Shipwreck

On June 7, 1928, steaming from the Windigo dock, Captain Smith turned *America*'s command over to First Mate John Wick and retired to his cabin. Five minutes later, the ship scraped a reef, tearing a hole through her single hull. Five lifeboats rescued all passengers except one pet dog. Fishing families still speak fondly of wooden crates of lemons, oranges, apples, and strawberries, preserved by the cold water and salvaged for the rest of the summer.

The *America* prow now lies just four feet below its buoy in the North Gap. Through calm water, its foredeck, capstans, the dark rectangles of deck hatches, windlasses, and eighty feet of her port and starboard gunwales are visible before they vanish into the watery depths.

Washington Harbor's Outer Islands

Through the North Gap from Washington Harbor, we turned west, along Thompson Island's north shore. Smooth swells, oily gray in the evening's dim twilight, surged around black basalt rock. Our bodies felt the distances: 14 empty miles to Canada's shore; 200 feet of icy water beneath our hulls.

Thompson Island Shore

Most paddlers bypass far-flung Washington, Thompson, and Johns Islands west of Washington Harbor. But the black basalt of Thompson and Johns Islands' north and west coasts are scoured by Lake Superior storms. Their sheer cliffs, pocket caves, and fairy arches are the rarely exposed bottoms of the Portage Lake Volcanic flows. They create a unique Isle Royale topography.

Washington Island Cottage

As you round either Johns or Thompson Islands' western ends, Washington, Barnum, Booth, and Grace Island smudge the southern horizon ahead. Washington Island, Portage Lake, Grace Island, and Greenstone volcanic lava flows, originally laid flat, now sit nearly vertical, side-by-side like books on a shelf.

Sam and Art Sivertson established the first commercial fishing operation on Washington Island in the early 1890s. The Sivertson name on a wooden plank labels the dock constructed more than a century ago. You are welcome to land and wander among the houses, boats, and commercial fishing artifacts. Sunset Point lies due north of the Sivertson residence. The prominent, waist-high boulder that punctuates the grassed meadow has provided the Isle Royale baseline survey benchmark since the 1800s.

Walter Singer constructed a two-story, framed Island House Hotel on Washington Island in 1902, along with ten cottages scattered along the lake shore, and a recreational hall with a bowling alley that doubled as a dance floor. He built a dock to accommodate his new, two-hundred passenger ship, the *Iroquois*, and other passenger boats like the *America*. A steel structure boosted a radio antenna above Isle Royale's ridges, allowing Singer to communicate with his mainland businesses and ships plying Lake Superior.

Washington Island Radio Tower

Five of the Singer Resort cottages, fish houses, net houses, the Sivertson residence, docks, and a collection of fishing equipment remain on Washington Island. Ramble among the nets, buoys, fish boxes, floats, and boats sitting where they were last hauled out a half century ago. Hike the shore to the island's east end and climb a rise of sixty feet to stand below the radio tower's steel beams. If the *Picnic*, a resort cruising launch built in 1949 by Reuben Hill, is berthed near the Sivertson dock, take a moment to admire her meticulously maintained wood, gleaming brass rails, and the high seat from which its captain still steers a watchful crossing from the North Shore.

The North Gap to Huginnin Cove

Whitecaps crisscrossed Washington Harbor. Wind and waves picked up as I rounded into the North Gap and then quieted in Thompson Island's lee. But on open Lake Superior, waves were three feet. The wind, now behind me, was seventeen knots. Ahead, the horizon stretched to a thin blue line—the Canadian coast. For as far as I could see, in every direction, there were no fishing boats, no trails, not a house nor a power line. Only rock and water and the shore's thick forest. I might've been the only person on the planet.

Three coves pierced the rock beyond the North Gap. If waves felt too big, I planned to take shelter in one of them. In different conditions, that plan might have worked. But today's waves drove directly into each cove's rocky arms. They slammed into the back cliffs with a reverberating roar.

I scanned the middle cove for landings. Near its back was a narrow strip of either flat rock or gravel. As I pulled closer, waves surfed my boat. Hitting a narrow gravel band, partly blocked by a fallen tree, I popped my skirt, scrambled out, and rushed to tug a hundred-fifty pounds of boat and gear above the next wave before it could fill its cockpit.

Adrenaline saturated every cell as I dragged the dry suit zipper from waist to shoulder and turtled out of its latex neck. Was I crazy? There was absolutely no reason not to turn back into the protected Washington Harbor. I grabbed a water bottle and a snack bar, scrambled up four feet of soft sand at the back of the narrow beach and followed a moose trail to gnarled roots among thick moss at the base of a towering cedar to consider my options.

Three shallow bays rimmed with basalt and skinny gravel beaches notch Isle Royale's western end between the North Gap and McGinty Cove. You are only an hour's paddle from Windigo, where a historic wooden Mackinaw boat docks next to sailing sloops and two-story pleasure cruisers. Where you can flush a toilet, place a satellite phone call, or buy an ice-cream cone. But squeeze between the North Gap's soaring cliffs, glide over the prow of the wrecked SS *America*, and you enter another world. Low mountains behind Lake Superior's north shore sweep a thin blue band across 270 degrees. Between you and that shore is fourteen miles of frigid and empty, undulating water.

The energy of Lake Superior swells concentrates as they move into the bays' crescent embrace. Waves steepen over shallow bottoms. Surf's white lace breaks over barely submerged rock or splays against glistening black cliffs reaching thin fingers from the shore. Waves glide into shallow sea caves, explode with a giant's glug against their back wall, and flow back in confused clapotis.

Past McGinty Cove, there are no landings for 1.5 miles. Nestled behind fingers of the Hill Point lava flow is Huginnin Cove's gravel beach. Straight back is the landing nearest the one close campsite.

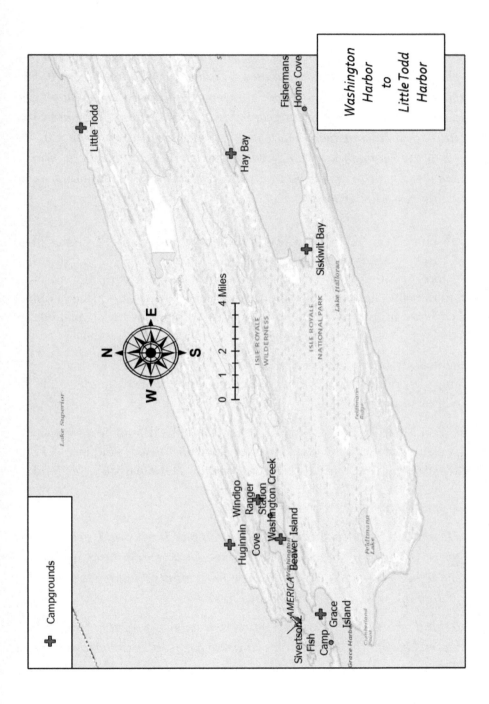

Washington
Harbor
to
Little Todd
Harbor

Campgrounds

Little Todd

Hay Bay

Fishermans
Home Cove

Siskiwit Bay

Lake Halloran

Lake Superior

N
W   E
S

0   1   2   4 Miles

ISLE ROYALE
WILDERNESS

ISLE ROYALE
NATIONAL PARK

Feldtmann Ridge

Feldtmann
Lake

Windigo
Ranger
Station
Washington Creek

Huginnin
Cove

Beaver Island

AMERICA Washington Harbor

Sivertson
Fish
Camp

Grace
Island

Grace Harbor

Cumberland
Point

Huginnin Cove to Little Todd Harbor

Burrowed in my sleeping bag, I raised an arm to lift my VHF radio to the precise angle that would capture a Canadian weather forecast. The forecast predicted southeast winds to veer to the northwest by noon and build to twenty knots. Would I make the twelve miles from Huginnin Cove to Little Todd Harbor before that wind pounded waves onto the cliffs? I felt restless to launch on what seemed like perfect paddling conditions. But each moment of indecision cut into the weather window and made launching more ill-advised.

The distance from Huginnin Cove to Little Todd Harbor is 13 miles. The first 11 miles trace vertical cliffs of the Hill Point lava flow. Ten faults slice this shore, creating gaps barely wider than a kayak length. Twenty feet behind the cliff face, each slice plunges to a steep slope of polished cobble. Waves have swept any stone smaller than a fist from these high-energy beaches.

Sunlight does not penetrate these narrow rock slashes. On calm seas, landing is an option. But with waves, entering them and landing would be difficult or impossible.

Little Todd Harbor breaks the Hill Point flow cliffs. Basalt crops out at the back of the harbor. Alluvium, however, provides beach landings at Little Todd's east and west ends. The campground is at the harbor's west end.

Little Todd Harbor to McCargoe Cove

The day was overcast and cool. I landed on Little Todd Harbor's east corner, strung a tarp, set up a chair, changed into dry clothing, and boiled water for hot ginger tea. I would settle here until surf stopped pounding spray high up rocks of the Hill Point Flow.

Behind the beach, fewmets marked a moose's route. Pine, black swamp muck, and the thick humus of decaying wood perfumed the air. A nodding wood nymph's five cream petals climbed inches above the moss. A spike of round-leafed orchid's pale green flowers rose from a single,

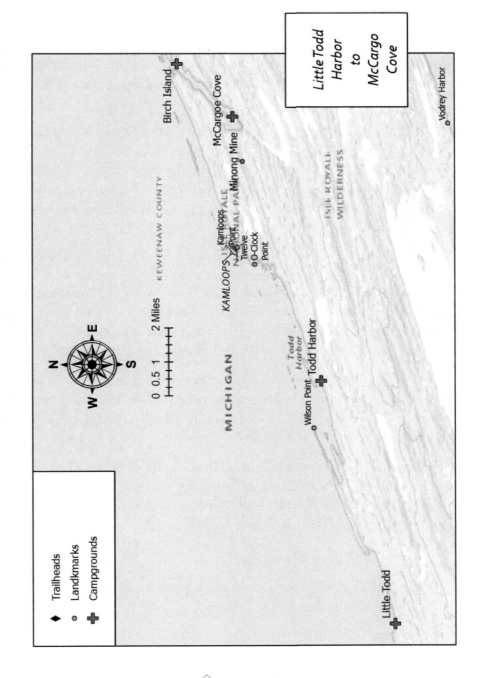

Little Todd
Harbor
to
McCargo
Cove

Birch Island

McCargoe Cove

Minong Mine

KEWEENAW COUNTY

Kamloops
Point

KAMLOOPS ISLE ROYALE
NATIONAL PA

Twelve
O-Clock
Point

ISLE ROYALE
WILDERNESS

Vodrey Harbor

MICHIGAN

Todd
Harbor

Todd Harbor

Wilson Point

Little Todd

N
W   E
S

0 0.5 1   2 Miles

Trailheads
Landkmarks
Campgrounds

two-lobed basal leaf. Birds chittered. I imagined they discussed the strange creature wearing smooth, nylon feathers.

When I finally launched, I was focused on the waves. Cliffs offered no landing. I'd seen only three boats, all on the distant horizon. While confident I could handle these conditions, if I needed a rescue, it would have to be my own.

From Little Todd Harbor, the Isle Royale shore follows the Hill Point flow for 11.25 miles to McCargoe Cove. Except in Todd Harbor, there are no landing options. Wilson Point marks the west end of Todd Harbor's mouth. Rounding the point, a large promontory looms over the harbor's backshore. The Todd Harbor Campground is south of this promontory, on its west side.

Todd Harbor's northeast end is Twelve O'clock Point, the time that the *America*'s Captain Smith needed to pass this spot to stay on schedule. Another half mile northeast of 12 O'clock Point is Kamloops Point. In December 1927, the 260-foot *Kamloops* disappeared in a blinding snowstorm. For more than a half century, her disappearance remained a mystery until divers discovered her in these deep waters in 1979.

From Kamloops Point to McCargoe Cove, the shore runs straight along a Hill Point lava flow cliff. A bit more than halfway along this route, Hawk Island runs parallel and 0.2 miles from the Isle Royale shore. Its south shore is a landing option.

Turning into McCargoe Cove, the Huginnin flow creates a long reef across its mouth. Birch Island and the entrance to Brady Cove are 0.25 miles inside. The Birch Island Campground is located on Birch Island's southwest corner. The McCargoe Cove Campground is another 1.9 miles.

McCargoe Cove to Rock Harbor

Middle and Gateway Journey paddling route descriptions complete your Committed Circumnavigation Journey.

Hikes

Southwestern Isle Royale sports fewer hiking trails and they are less used. Below are descriptions of some that are accessible to paddlers and make interesting day trips.

Island Mine Trail

The Island Mine Trail begins at the Siskiwit Bay Campground and circles the west end of Siskiwit Bay for 1.5 miles. Bridges span two forks of the Big Siskiwit River before the trail crosses Senter Point's neck.

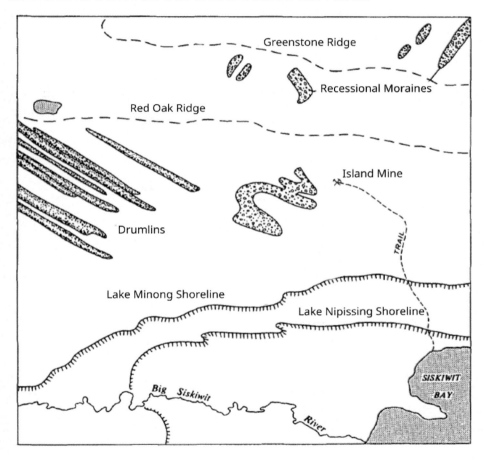

West Siskiwit Bay Glacial Features from Huber

Between the trail and the point are stone remains of a powder house, where the Island Mining Company stored explosives in the 1870s.

The next half mile skirts Carnelian Beach, named for the semitransparent red gemstones found here. The Island Mine company town was located where the trail turns inland. Past the Siskiwit Bay shore, the trail follows the wagon road that transported 213,345 pounds of copper between 1874 and 1878. Its Island Mine source is another 2 miles.

As the trail climbs, spruce, fir, and paper birch give way to sugar maples, yellow birch, and northern red oaks. Look for an old well 1.6 miles from Siskiwit Bay. The Island Mine Campground is 0.7 miles past the mine site. Another half mile brings you to the Greenstone Ridge Trail junction.

Feldtmann Ridge Trail

On a southwest nob of Isle Royale, this trail is far from the well-used Greenstone and Minong Ridge Trails. When Isle Royale wolves were more numerous, a pack prowled this remote territory.

From Siskiwit Bay Campground, the Feldtmann Ridge Trail skirts Big Siskiwit River swamp for 3.5 miles before climbing the north slope of Coyote Ridge. The Feldtmann Tower is 5.4 miles from the campground. Trees have grown up around the tower, and there is no view. Beyond the tower, the trail descends another 4.8 miles through birch and mountain ash to the Feldtmann Lake Campground.

Feldtmann Lake Trail

Feldtmann Lake Trail begins at Windigo. The first 1.2 miles traces the Washington Harbor shore with views of Beaver Island. The trail continues southwest for another 4.3 miles before turning east and following a contour between Lake Superior and Feldtmann Lake. The total trail distance from Windigo to Feldtmann Lake is 8.5 miles. A half-mile trail from Rainbow Cove will intersect the Feldtmann Lake Trail at the campground.

Washington Creek Trail

The Washington Creek Trail begins at the Washington Creek Campground, east of the Windigo dock. It intersects the Greenstone Ridge Trail in 0.3 miles. The trail passes a streamflow gauging station at the Washington Creek bridge. At 0.6 miles, it tees with the West Huginnin and Minong Ridge Trails. Lady's slippers bloom along this short trail on June and early July days. Moose are frequently seen in the Washington Creek marsh.

West Huginnin Trail

West and East Huginnin Trails join at the Huginnin Cove Campground to make a 7-mile loop that includes 0.6 miles of the Minong Ridge Trail. From the campground, the West Huginnin Cove Trail follows a southerly fault that connects Huginnin Cove and Washington Harbor. It crosses Huginnin Creek near the campground and climbs a short ridge of Portage Lake Volcanic flow before dropping to cross a marsh, skirt the base of Minong Ridge, and wrap around an unnamed ridge that rises 160 feet above Washington Harbor.

East Huginnin Trail

Beach Along East Huginnin Trail

The East Huginnin Cove Trail skirts the cove's east shore and Isle Royale's north shore. This trail section offers views of Lake Superior and the Canadian shore, flat rocks, and private beaches for sunbathing. It may be possible to bounce text messages or even a phone call off Canadian cell towers from here.

After tracing the Isle Royale shore for 1 mile, the East Huginnin Cove Trail turns south and then east to follow an inland ridge. It crosses a swamp and skirts a lake, both excellent locations for viewing wildlife.

The Wendigo Mine site, established in 1890, lies 3 miles from the campground. The mine and its two settlements quickly failed. But steel rails, a relic log cabin wall, and copper mine pits hide among the vegetation. Do not enter the mine pits.

Beyond the remnant mine site, the trail wraps round another swamp and begins climbing the Minong Ridge Trail. The West Huginnin Cove Trail intersects the Minong Ridge Trail 0.6 miles southwest of the East Huginnin Cove Trail.

Campgrounds
Hay Bay Campground

Seven miles from the Malone Bay Campground, Hay Bay Campground lies behind Hay Point in Siskiwit Bay. Protected from Siskiwit Bay conditions, the sheltered cove hosted commercial fishing families in the early 1900s. There is a boat dock and a single tent site. It's reportedly a good place to see moose, though I've never seen one there. There is, however, an abundance of mosquitoes. The June 1 to Labor Day stay limit is three nights.

Siskiwit Bay Campground

 Nestled into the western end of Siskiwit Bay, warmer air and water have earned this campground a "Riviera of Isle Royale" designation. The campground provides access to the Island Mine and Feldtmann Ridge Trails. It is 6 miles beyond the Hay Bay Campground, and visiting this camp adds about 7 miles of paddling to a direct crossing from Hay Point to Point Houghton. The campground has two shelters, four tent sites, three group sites, and a boat dock. The June 1 to Labor Day stay limit is three nights.

Backcountry Camps

Hay Bay Campground to Grace Island Campground is a paddling distance of about 25.5 miles. A cross-country permit authorizes your group to camp along this shore. Note that your camp must be at least 200 feet (75 paces) from all water bodies, including Lake Superior, and not visible from the water or any other campers. No fires are permitted. The maximum stay at a location is one night.

Suitable landings for camping access include Little Boat Harbor (2.3 miles from Point Houghton), Attwood Beach (6.2 miles from Point Houghton), a small, unnamed lake seventy-five feet from Lake Superior (11 miles from Point Houghton), beaches east or west of Long Point (12 miles from Point Houghton), a beach west of the Head (14.3 miles from Point Houghton), and Rainbow Cove (16.6 miles from Point Houghton).

While these locations offer landings on gravel beaches, establishing a camp in the woods or swamp behind the beach may be challenging. The ground is likely to be rough and overgrown. In many places, it is swampy. You may have to heave gear bags up steep beach slopes. A relic ancestral lake gravel beach makes an ideal campsite.

At Rainbow Cove, there is a small clearing behind the beach at the trailhead to Feldtmann Lake. Feldtmann Lake Campground is another option, if you are willing to haul your gear a half mile along a flat trail.

Grace Island Campground

Grace Island Campground is on the northeast side of Grace Island. The site has two shelters and a boat dock. The best landing for kayaks is a beach in front of Shelter #2. In 2021, gaps in the screen and door frame, however, meant that Shelter #2 was not secure from mosquitoes or small deer mice, who are wise to the world of granola, chocolate bars, and cheese.

A short trail north from Shelter #1 follows the beach to a gravel spit reaching into the channel between Grace and Washington Harbors. Wild irises bloom here in June and early July. The Grace Island Campground June 1 to Labor Day stay limit is three nights.

Beaver Island Campground

Shelter #3 was farthest from the boat dock, with a pebble beach perfect for landing and a foot-high lift onto a grass patch. A fallen aspen branch offered a footrest over a smoochy kiss of water on poorly sorted, polished stone. Raven's caw punctuated voices from the Feldtmann Lake Trail on Washington Harbor's south shore.

Washington Harbor bustled after the isolation of Isle Royale's north shore. Motorboats steamed past. Seaplanes zipped along its channel. A chipmunk scampered across my chart, scouting for neglected bits of nuts or dried fruit.

Beaver Island nestles into the head of Washington Harbor, just 0.8 miles from the Windigo dock. There are three shelters, each facing the water. Shelter #3, farthest from the dock, has the best kayak landing, a gravel beach, three bums wide, from which you can lift a boat bow onto the grass. The June 1 to Labor Day stay limit is three nights.

Washington Creek Campground

The Washington Creek Campground is 0.3 miles from the Windigo Ranger Station dock. Leave your boat at the dock. Use the cart to trundle your gear. East and West Huginnin, Feldtmann Lake, Minong, and Greenstone Ridge Trails are accessible from the campground. There are ten shelters, five tent sites, and four group sites. The June 1 to Labor Day stay limit is three nights.

The *Voyager II* docks at Windigo on its way to and from the Hat Marina on the Minnesota shore. Above the dock are the Visitors Center, the Windigo Store, flush toilets, laundry, and potable water. Rustic cabins are also available to rent.

Shortly after executing agreements with Lake Superior's Ojibwe, the United States granted five thousand acres of western Isle Royale to the Wendigo Copper Company in 1890. The company constructed the Ghyllbank settlement on the Washington Harbor shore. Besides sixty miners, Ghyllbank's 135 residents included school-aged children, toddlers, and infants. The community's physician also taught school and staffed the customs office. Sheds, storehouses, and an imposing two-story headquarters were constructed, and forest was cleared for a vegetable garden and hay pasture.

The Wendigo Copper Company diamond-drilled sixteen boreholes hrough the hard basalt of Isle Royale's north shore to as deep as 1,038 feet. Geologists still rely on information from these borings to confirm relationships between Isle Royale and Keweenaw Peninsula basalt flows. But the copper quality was poor, and its location was too remote to be profitable.

When the Wendigo Copper Company failed, it sold land and the settlement buildings for tourist homes and resorts. A private Duluth sporting club purchased its two-story headquarters.

Huginnin Cove Campground

Huginnin Cove Campground is 8 miles from the Windigo dock. It has five tent sites, but Lake Superior waves long ago pounded its dock into oblivion. Landing is on a wide gravel beach. The June 1 to Labor Day stay limit is three nights.

Thimbleberry Leaves Left For You

Most of Isle Royale's campground pit toilets are constructed of painted plywood. But Huginnin Cove features an older design built from weathered one-by-ten planks. Light penetrates narrow slits between each plank. These older toilets have no paper, not even a holder. Despite three furry thimbleberry leaves left for you on the floor, you may want to bring your own.

The Huginnin Cove Trail is a beautiful stroll from the campground. In the right season, pink lady's slipper flowers bloom along its edges.

Little Todd Harbor Campground

Little Todd Harbor Campground is on Little Todd Harbor's western end. There is no dock. A wide stone beach provides a landing. There are four tent sites. This campground is the northeast end of the committed 11.5-mile paddle from Huginnin Cove. The June 1 to Labor Day stay limit is two nights.

Todd Harbor Campground

The Todd Harbor Campground is tucked behind a basalt nub, 5.7 miles from Little Todd Harbor. It is 0.1 miles from the Minong Ridge Trail. It has a boat dock, five tent sites, and three group sites. The June 1 to Labor Day stay limit is three nights.

Between Todd Harbor and Hay Bay Campgrounds

The Gateway and Middle Journey sections describe campgrounds between Todd Harbor and Hay Bay.

Leaving

Years later, none of the cells of this physical form carried a boat from the ferry dock to launch on a rocky shore. None of "me" leaned against a log wall of the Wright Island cabin. But I continue to live by lessons from my first Isle Royale solo paddle.

Responsive to wind, waves, rain, light, rock, and desire, I learned to decide less in advance and lean more into each moment. I learned to step carefully. To wait for an opening. I learned that my mind fears an idea, but seated in my boat, I am rarely afraid. There is no guardian angel, but I am held in my journey in ways that surprise me.

Congratulations! You are one of us who carry forward the Isle Royale/Minong paddling tradition. You've touched and been touched by billion-year-old basalt. You've disconnected from distractions and allowed your nervous system to synchronize with ancient rhythms of sunlight and darkness, with the fluttering quake of aspen leaves, with the pulse of waves against the shore.

Now, before you climb on your ferry, in this state of tender connectedness, take a moment to harvest your trip. Clean those stones from your pockets. They cannot carry what you want to bring home. What were your satisfactions? Lessons? Discoveries? Wins? What were disappointments and frustrations? What are you grateful for? What are you taking with you? What are you leaving behind?

Many of us will return to Isle Royale. For some of us this will be our last trip. It is a gift to have made an Isle Royale kayaking journey even once.

Bibliography

Isle Royale Guidebooks

DuFresne, Jim. Isle Royale National Park: Foot Trails & Water Routes, Fifth Edition. Clarkston, Michigan: MichiganTrailMaps.com, 2020.

Natural History

Gostomski, Ted and Marr, Janet. Island Life: An Isle Royale Nature Guide. Houghton, Michigan: Isle Royale Natural History Association, 2007.

Huber, N. King. The Geologic Story of Isle Royale National Park. Revised by Isle Royale Natural History Association in cooperation with the National Park Service and the Geological Survey. Formerly U.S. Geological Survey Bulletin 1309. Marquette, Michigan: United States Department of the Interior, Geological Survey, 1983[1996].

Lynch, Bob and Lynch, Dan. Lake Superior Rocks & Minerals: A Field Guide to the Lake Superior Area. Cambridge, Minnesota: Adventure Publications, Inc., 2008.

Peterson, Rolf O. The Wolves of Isle Royale: A Broken Balance. Ann Arbor: The University of Michigan Press, 2007.

Walewski, Joe. Lichens of the North Woods: A field guide to 111 northern lichens. Duluth, Minnesota: Kollath+Stensaas Publishing, 2007.

Peterson, Carolyn C. A View From the Wolf's Eye. Houghton, Michigan: Isle Royale Natural History Association, 2008.

Ojibwe History and Stories

Broker, Ignatia. Night Flying Woman: An Ojibwe Narrative. United States of America: Borealis Books, Minnesota Historical Society Press, 1983.

Cochrane, Timothy. Minong—The Good Place: Ojibwe and Isle Royale. East Lansing, Michigan: Michigan State University Press, 2009.

Johnston, Basil. The Manitous: The Supernatural World of the Ojibway. Toronto, Canada: Key Porter Books Limited, 1995.

Colonizer History

Baldwin, Amalia Tholen. Becoming Wilderness: Nature, History, and the Making of Isle Royale National Park. Houghton, Michigan: Isle Royale & Keweenaw Parks Association, 2011.

Cochrane, Timothy and Tolson, Hawk. A Good Boat Speaks for Itself: Isle Royale Fishermen and Their Boats. Minneapolis, Minnesota: University of Minnesota Press, 2002.

Gale, Thomas P. and Gale, Kendra L. Isle Royale: A Photographic History. Houghton, Michigan: Isle Royale Natural History Association, 1995.

Harmon, David (editor). Borealis: An Isle Royale Potpourri. Hancock, Michigan: Isle Royale Natural History Association, 1992.

Holte, Ingebord. Ingeborg's Isle Royale. Grand Marais, Minnesota: Women's Times Publishing, 1984 [1989].

Oikarinen, Peter. Island Folk: The People of Isle Royale. Minneapolis, Minnesota: University of Minnesota Press, 2008.

Parratt, Smitty and Welker, Doug. The Place Names of Isle Royale. Houghton, Michigan: Isle Royale Natural History Association, 1999.

Poirier, Jessica J. and Taylor, Richard E. Images of America: Isle Royale. United States of America: Arcadia Publishing, 2007.

Seglem, Elling. Robert Root and Jill Burkland (editors). Diaries of an Isle Royale Fisherman. Hancock, Michigan: Isle Royale Natural History Association, 2002.

Simonson, Dorothy. The Diary of an Isle Royale School Teacher: A memoir of a winter on an isolated island in Lake Superior during the Great Depression. Houghton, Michigan: Isle Royale Natural History Association, 1999.

Sivertson, Howard. Once Upon An Isle: The Story of Fishing Families on Isle Royale. Mount Horeb, Wisconsin: Wisconsin Folk Museum, 1992.

Kayaking and Expedition Planning

Anderson, Dave and Absolon, Molly. NOLS Expedition Planning. Mechanicsburg, Pennsylvania: Stackpole Books, 2011.

Burch, David. Fundamentals of Kayak Navigation. Chester, Connecticut: The Globe Pequote Press, 1987.

Collins, Loel. Kayak Rolling: The Black Art Demystified. Guilford, Connecticut: The Globe Pequote Press, 2009.

Cooper, Doug. Rough Water Handling. Caernarfon, Gwynedd: Pesda Press, 2012.

Dowd, John. Sea Kayaking: A Manual for Long-Distance Touring. Vancouver, British Columbia: Douglas & McIntyre Ltd., 1988.

Isaac, Jeff, P.A.-C and Goth, Peter, M.D. The Outward-Bound Wilderness First-Aid Handbook. New York, New York, Lyons & Burford, 1991.

Isle Royale Fiction

Barr, Nevada. A Superior Death. New York: Berkley, 2003.

Barr, Nevada. Winter Study. New York: Berkley, 2009.

Campbell, Loraine. A Pocketful of Passage. Detroit, Michigan: Wayne State University Press, 2007.

Curtis, Rebecca S. Charlotte Avery on Isle Royale. Mount Horeb, Wisconsin: Midwest Traditions, Inc., 1995.

Resources

Find a packing list, GPS coordinates, species list, geologic map, and other resources at KayakIsleRoyale.com/resources.

Packing List

Clothing	3 pairs synthetic underwear		Kitchen	pot scraper	
	synthetic base layer			quart and gallon zip-top bags	
	nylon long-sleeved shirt			shower/hand wash	
	nylon pants			soap	
	cotton t-shirt			pots and skillet	
	lightweight fleece jacket			stove w/ heat shield & screen	
	fleece pants			fuel	
	rain pants			spatula	
	wet or dry suit			water filter	
	paddling jacket			water bottle or bladder	
	storm cag			iodine	
Head	Shade hat			matches and/or lighters	
	warm hat			cup, plate, spoon, fork, knife	
	mosquito net		Health & Safety	car key	
Hands	lightweight warm gloves			head lamp and spare batteries	
	paddling gloves			chart & map	
Feet	3 pair wool socks			sunglasses and strap	
	trail shoes			multi-purpose tool	
	boat shoes			GPS	
	sandals			1st aid kit	
Boat	boat			whistle	
	hatch covers			paracord	
	spray skirt			pump	
	Paddle & spare			tow belt	
	life jacket			VHF radio	
	Pump & sponge			repair kit	

Shelter	Tent			Camera	
	Tarp			Swim suit	
	Sleeping bag w waterproof, compressible sack			Binoculars	
	Sleeping pad			Carabiners	
Toiletries	toothpaste & brush		Extras	Pen, ink, & journal	
	sunscreen			Field guides	
	lip balm			Clothespins	
	hand lotion			Daypack	
	camp towel			Camp chair	
	comb			Soft-side lunchbox	
	soap			Solar charger	
	bug repellent			bandana	
Latrine	spade for cathole				
	toilet paper				

Landmark GPS Coordinates

An electronic copy is available on KayakIsleRoyale.com/resources

	Latitude	Longitude
Campgrounds		
Beaver Island	47.90572	-89.17156
Belle Isle	48.15233	-88.58515
Birch Island	48.11006	-88.68525
Caribou Island	48.09513	-88.57191
Chippewa Harbor	48.02888	-88.65038
Daisy Farm	48.09221	-88.59469
Duncan Bay	48.15029	-88.52159
Duncan Narrows	48.16932	-88.47828
Grace Island	47.88271	-89.21624
Hay Bay	47.93423	-88.94071
Huginnin Cove	47.93500	-89.17485
Lane Cove	48.14490	-88.55720
Little Todd	48.02053	-88.92544
Malone Bay	47.98490	-88.80557
McCargoe Cove	48.08715	-88.70789
Merritt Lane	48.18463	-88.42979
Moskey Basin	48.06295	-88.64453
Pickerel Cove	48.12387	-88.65252
Rock Harbor	48.14517	-88.48970
Siskiwit Bay	47.89081	-88.99804
Three Mile	48.12394	-88.52988

	Latitude	Longitude
Campgrounds		
Todd Harbor	48.05081	-88.82186
Tookers Island	48.12943	-88.50328
Washington Creek	47.91876	-89.14821
Geographical Points	Latitude	Longitude
Attwood Beach	47.86265	-89.01424
Blake Point	48.19097	-88.42203
Blueberry Cove	48.01171	-88.67402
Kamloops Point	48.08509	-88.76442
Locke Point	48.18429	-88.45926
Long Point	47.82781	-89.11920
Middle Islands Passage	48.09266	-88.57476
Point Houghton	47.90225	-88.89924
Rainbow Cove	47.84184	-89.19200
Saginaw Point	48.06077	-88.57613
Schooner Island	47.98410	-88.75497
Scoville Point	48.16322	-88.44910
Smithwick Channel	48.13833	-88.48126
Snug Harbor	48.14578	-88.48426
The Head	47.82364	-89.15799
Twelve O-Clock Point	48.07813	-88.77154
Vodrey Harbor	47.99834	-88.71083
Wilson Point	48.05397	-88.84187

	Latitude	Longitude
Historical Points of Interest		
Wright Island Fish Camp	47.96866	-88.83182
Amygdaloid Ranger Station	48.13575	-88.65576
Bangsund Cabin	48.08736	-88.59019
Captain Kidd Fish Camp	48.16642	-88.56717
Crystal Cove Fish Camp	48.15881	-88.59050
Edisen Fishery	48.08983	-88.58291
Fishermans Home Cove	47.89173	-88.91385
Minong Mine	48.08319	-88.72720
Mount Ojibway Tower	48.10846	-88.60652
Sivertson Fish Camp	47.87657	-89.23323
Windigo Ranger Station	47.91187	-89.15783
	Latitude	Longitude
Lighthouses		
Isle Royale Lighthouse	47.94788	-88.76130
Rock Harbor Lighthouse	48.08991	-88.57907
	Latitude	Longitude
Trailheads		
Amygdaloid Arch	48.14967	-88.61947
Duncan Portage North	48.15487	-88.50337
Duncan Portage South	48.14921	-88.49598
Five Finger Bay Portage	48.15614	-88.51778
Hidden Lake	48.15868	-88.47177
Lane Cove Portage	48.14866	-88.55100

	Latitude	*Longitude*
Docks		
Mott Island Dock	48.10746	-88.54585
Queen IV Dock	47.47015	-87.89191
Ranger III Dock	47.12326	-88.56400
Raspberry Island Dock	48.14211	-88.47538
Rock Harbor Marina	48.14566	-88.48619
Tobin Harbor Dock	48.14790	-88.48560
Voyager II Dock	47.96242	-89.65276

Acknowledgements

Not even solo paddlers make any journey alone. I am profoundly grateful to the people who've made my journeys possible. My Isle Royale paddling companions have been David, Eamon, and Geneva White, Ava Kovach, Mary Hatch, Claire Fitzpatrick, Lisa Fithian, Jim Yazvec, Patti and Niles, Pat Yingst, Tony Patchman, Mohan Rao, Elizabeth Kubala, Donna Hoffman, and Lee Cohen. Each of you are woven through every word of this book. I love you all.

I am grateful for the competent and generous kayaking coaches who've uprighted my failed rolls, kept an eye toward the sea as I entered slots, and encouraged me to go where I'd never dared without you. Alec and Sharon Bloyd-Peshkin with Have Kayaks Will Travel, Trey Rouse and Scott Fairty at Power of Water, you each rock my world.

Thank you to Amy Bee at Lion By the Tail for reading and editing the roughest of drafts. My Self-Publishing School coach, Ellaine Ursuy kept me on course through this book-writing journey. Without her and the Self-Publishing School staff, I'd still be at sea, a million miles from finished. Find them at SelfPublishingSchool.com.

ABOUT THE AUTHOR

Juniper Lauren made her first kayak trip to Isle Royale in 1991. She's returned more than a dozen times since, with friends and family from two to seventy-two. She's made four solo trips and circumnavigated Isle Royale twice. She holds PaddleSports' Three-Star certificate in ocean kayaking. When she's not on Lake Superior, find her on the water near her home in  Austin, Texas, scouting shores for ripe wild cherries.

Printed in Great Britain
by Amazon

10457056R00108